Pestos! Cooking With Herb Pastes

by Dorothy Rankin

✳ THE CROSSING PRESS / FREEDOM, CALIFORNIA 95019

Library of Congress Cataloging-in-Publication Data
Rankin, Dorothy.
      Pestos! : cooking with herb pastes.
      Includes index.
      1. Pestos.   I. Title.
TX819.P45R36   1985   641.6'38   85-17121
ISBN 0-89594-180-5 (pbk.)

To my mother, Mary,
and all the Packards,
who sure knew how to cook

My thanks go to friends and family who enabled me to stay with this project: Laurie Pettibon, for her creative ideas, unwavering support and invaluable typing; Andrea Chesman, my editor and friend, for her guidance, faith, and encouragement; Linda Mansfield, for her continuing interest and support in sharing the dream; Pam Durda, for generously sharing herbal information; Patty Brushett, whose enthusiasm and friendship lightened the load; Troye Mackie, up and coming Providence chef, for sharing creative ideas; Daune Peckham and Sally Bevins, for sharing their herbal delights; Sally Turpin, of The Net Result, for answering all of my questions; and Mary Collin, who told me I had to do it.

Contents

Preface

It is said, "He who eats pesto never leaves Genoa."

A Genoese pesto is undoubtedly one of the world's great culinary pleasures. Made from fresh basil leaves, pale green oil from ripe olives, a local sharp sheep's cheese, garlic cloves, and pine nuts, this sublime essence is especially savored during the lush summer months.

In Genoa, where pesto originated, fresh basil is available year-round. The name, "pesto," derives from the pestle. Today, the food processor and blender have replaced the mortar and pestle, but the intense flavors of the fresh herbs are retained. The freezer has made it possible to store quantities of pesto for enjoyment year-round, making those superb flavors as easily available in January as in August.

But not only can you enjoy pesto year-round, you can also enjoy a whole range of herb pastes made by combining various different herbs, fresh greens, oils, and nuts.

The variables in a "classic" basil pesto are many. There are no givens when it comes to making pestos in Genoa or in other provinces of Italy. No two towns make it the same way. Some versions include cream, other pestos call for butter. Pine nuts (pignolia) are a later addition to pesto. A Genoa pesto may contain all Sardo Pecorino cheese (made from sheep's milk), whereas in this country, we usually combine a Romano Pecorino and Parmesan cheese or make a pesto with all Parmesan. As Ed Giobbi said in his book *Italian Family Cooking,* "When I was in Genoa, I tried to find the truly authentic version (of pesto), but that experience convinced me that there is no such thing."

This book contains a very "classic" version of pesto and recipes that use the pesto as a seasoning. There are also some rather unusual pestos, using such diverse herbs as cilantro, rosemary, mint, and lemon thyme.

Why herb pastes? Because they add new flavor to foods. Once made and frozen or refrigerated, it is easy to add a tablespoon or two to a soup, sautéed vegetables, or some other dish in progress. While pesto and pasta make a perfect combination, combined with the juices of meat or fish, pesto makes a marvelous basting sauce. With the addition of a little milk or cream, you have an elegant sauce for pasta, fish, chicken, or vegetables.

The recipes presented here are both simple and elegant — all good food. The pestos are made from a variety of herbs, greens, oils, nuts, and cheeses. There is nothing complicated about the recipes or the process of making the herb pastes.

I hope that these recipes will be used as suggestions and inspiration for cooking with herbs. Adapt the recipes to whatever is fresh and good in your area. Fine fresh ingredients should always be the starting point, as the food will only be as good as the ingredients going into it.

In creating a dish, take a quiet moment and contemplate the ingredients you are thinking of combining. Perhaps smell them and taste a little. Is there something else that might combine well? If you have a garden, what does it hold? Cooking can be a wonderfully renewing pleasure. If the senses are involved, preparing simple food and cooking it can become so much more than a routine chore.

There are really no givens in cooking or in these recipes so you must trust your culinary instincts. The herbs will vary in strength, taste, and flavors, depending on the seed, the soil, the weather, and when and how the herbs were picked. The garlic may be weak or strong, the oils and cheeses will vary. You, the cook, will gather all the ingredients together, taste, smell, and touch, devise a plan, and proceed. And, if you take pleasure in the process and use good, fresh ingredients, it will all be a success.

1.
Making Herb Pestos

From the beginning, let's understand that cooking is not an exact science. The amounts in any recipe are suggestions, and you must taste as you cook, and learn to respect and educate that sense of taste. Recipes are recommended formulas; but the ultimate results depend on using excellent fresh ingredients, getting involved and taking pleasure in the food, and continual tasting.

Making herb pestos definitely begins with selecting quality ingredients. Fresh basil leaves, garlic, freshly grated hard, sharp cheese, a good olive oil, and nuts comprise the basic pesto. This chapter also includes recipes for many different herb pestos, using tarragon, rosemary, and other fresh and dried herbs. The basic method of preparing a pesto doesn't vary, however.

Equipment

A handmade pesto, pounded in a mortar with a pestle, has a silky, chunky texture that cannot be duplicated in a machine. However, using a food processor or blend-er has simplified the time and effort in making pestos so much that I have no trouble using these machines.

I use the food processor for most of the fresh herb pestos, and the blender for making winter pestos, which are made with dried herbs. The tall, narrow container and blade of the blender facilitate breaking down the firm dried leaves of thyme and rosemary, which do not seem to combine well with the food processor blade. A blender-made pesto will have a puréed texture, but it is still a good sauce to make when fresh herbs are unavailable.

Herbs

Pick the leaves from the stem and measure the herb leaves first. Lightly pack the leaves in a measuring cup. Don't pack the leaves tightly. Measure before you wash.

To wash the leaves, immerse them in a bowl of cold water and swish them around. Drain in a strainer or colander and roll gently in a towel, or spin dry in a salad spinner. Fluff up the leaves and spread them on towels to dry further as you prepare the other ingredients.

When using herbs that don't provide a lot of green bulk, as with thyme, for example, you will have to add a "green extender." I prefer parsley for flavor, color, and texture (Italian flat parsley is the best); but spinach, kale, watercress, sorrel, and other greens will work well, too. Watercress adds a peppery flavor to a pesto, while sorrel gives it a lemony tang. The greens will dilute the flavor and intensity of the herb leaves, however. In the case of strongly flavored herbs, such as rosemary and thyme, this is desirable. With basil, there is no reason to weaken its good pungency. Parsley, and all greens, must be washed and well dried before being added to the pesto since water on the leaves will make the pesto runny.

In making winter pestos with dried herbs, it is crucial to use dried herbs that have a good strong aroma and are free of woody stems. (Thyme, in particular, should be picked free of stems.) Dried herbs have a short shelf life, 6 months at most, and should be replenished frequently. The flavor of the winter pestos is very dependent on the quality of the dried herbs.

Garlic

Good fresh garlic cloves are an integral component of this queen of sauces. Elephant garlic can be used; but since its flavor is considerably milder than regular garlic, adjust the number of cloves. The fresher the garlic, the better the flavor.

The garlic is combined with the herbs in the food processor when you make the pesto.

Cheese

Next, the cheese is added to the pesto. It must be freshly grated for full flavor. Buy the cheese in a chunk and grate it by hand or in the food processor with the grating disc, then the steel blade. I freeze extra grated cheese in small containers. Stored this way, grated cheese will retain its fresh flavor for up to 6 weeks, refrigerated or frozen.

Since Italian Sardo Pecorino is mostly unavailable at present in the United States, a blend of freshly grated Parmesan and Romano Pecorino seems to provide the best combination of sharpness and mellow flavor.

Oil

The choice of the right oil is most important in pesto. Olive oil, with its flavor and viscosity, is unequaled. A virgin olive oil, defined as a second-press oil, should provide sufficient quality. The strong flavor of the pesto overpowers the fruity extra virgin olive oil, although it will certainly make a fine pesto.

"Pure" olive oil can serve as an all-purpose oil, but it is not recommended for pestos. A "pure" olive oil is made from successive pressings of the leftover olive pulp. Often the oil is chemically extracted from the pits and pulp, or released in a hot water treatment.

Labeling of imported oils is not always accurate, and to date the FDA has not addressed this problem. Look for an oil that tastes of olives, without an aftertaste. When you find a good oil, buy it in small quantities. Cap it tightly and store it in a cool place. Heat and length of storage will affect the flavor.

I frequently buy an Italian second-press olive oil in bulk from a local health food store. It is a light oil and makes an excellent pesto. Because this store sells the oil in great quantities, I don't worry about buying a rancid oil that has sat on the shelf too long.

Nuts

Pine nuts, or pignolia, are a wonderful addition to the original pesto. You may prefer to toast the nuts lightly (5 minutes for pine nuts, 10 minutes for walnuts in a preheated 300°F. oven) before adding them to the pesto. I like the flavor of pestos with both the toasted and the untoasted nuts.

Walnuts taste quite satisfactory in a basil pesto, but the milder pine nuts or unsalted pistachios should be used in delicate pestos, such as a Tarragon Pesto. Sunflower seeds and pumpkin seeds can be used in pestos, also.

A pesto that contains discernible pieces of nuts is very pleasing. A handmade pesto usually will have this textured quality. You can achieve somewhat similar results by using the pulsing action in the food processor and processing just until the nuts are well mixed but not reduced to a smooth paste.

The Process

To make the traditional handmade pesto, you'll need a good-size marble mortar. Sprinkle some coarse sea salt or kosher salt and a few black peppercorns or freshly ground pepper from a mill into the mortar. Slice the garlic and add to the mortar. Pound the garlic, salt, and pepper together. The coarse salt will act as an abrasive to help purée the garlic and peppercorns. Add a few pine nuts and some basil leaves with a tablespoon of olive oil and continue pounding. Stir it all up occasionally. Add more leaves and nuts and a little oil. Continue crushing and stirring and adding the nuts, herbs, and a little oil. Too much oil will make it difficult to combine the ingre-

dients. When you have added all the nuts and basil and have a fairly smooth paste, add the freshly grated cheese and the remaining oil, a little at a time, until it is all incorporated into the pesto. You should have a thick purée. Taste for salt and season if needed. Let the pesto stand for a few minutes to allow the flavors to blend.

To make the pesto in a food processor, combine the herbs, whole garlic, grated cheese, and nuts in the bowl of the processor. Use the pulsing action to combine the ingredients. With the machine running, slowly add the olive oil. Turn the machine off, scrape down the sides of the bowl. Season to taste with salt and freshly ground pepper. The texture of the pesto will be fairly rough at this point. Continue to process until it reaches a good consistency — as smooth or as chunky as you wish. Use the pulsing action to prevent overprocessing.

An unusual pesto can be made by roughly chopping the herbs and nuts with a knife or mezzaluna (a two-handled knife with a blade shaped like a half-moon), or by using

5

the pulsing action of the food processor. Then mix in by hand the minced garlic, freshly grated cheese, and oil. The rough texture with the herbs and nuts still apparent makes a very pleasing sauce for pasta.

No matter by what method you make the pesto, allow it to stand for a few minutes before serving to allow the flavors to develop and blend. Just before serving or using it in a recipe, retaste and add salt and freshly ground pepper, if needed.

Storing Pestos

Pestos will keep well in the refrigerator for 3 or 4 weeks, if stored properly. Pack the pesto into a small container. Cover the pesto with a thin layer of olive oil and cap tightly. It is important to exclude as much air as possible to prevent loss of color and spoilage.

When you are ready to use the pesto, spoon out as much as you need. There will be some discoloration of the pesto on the surface, but this will not affect the flavor. Simply stir the discolored pesto into the green pesto below. Add to the layer of oil and refrigerate the remaining pesto.

Pestos can be frozen, also. Freeze it in small quantities to make it easy to thaw in just the amounts you need. You can freeze pesto in ½-cup or 1-cup plastic containers, covered tightly. It is not necessary to cover the pesto with a layer of oil when freezing. Or, freeze the pesto, by the heaping tablespoon, on baking sheets covered with waxed paper. When the pesto is frozen, place it in a plastic bag and store in the freezer.

Your pesto will taste fresher if it is frozen without the cheese, which can be added before serving. Craig Claiborne mentions that some Italian chefs feel pesto preserves better without salt. And, there are those who freeze pesto minus the nuts. I confess to sometimes freezing completely finished pesto and being satisfied with the results. The argument is ongoing.

You can freeze plain chopped basil in olive oil in small cups or in ice cube trays. Then store the small blocks of frozen basil and olive oil in plastic bags for later use. This method is a real time-saver for gardeners who raise their own basil and don't have time to make pesto for freezing.

Classic Basil Pesto

2 cups fresh basil leaves
2 large garlic cloves
1/2 cup freshly grated Parmesan
    cheese
2 tablespoons freshly grated
    Pecorino Romano cheese
1/4 cup pine nuts or walnuts
1/2 cup olive oil
Salt and freshly ground pepper

My version of a classic basil pesto includes a small portion of Pecorino Romano cheese. A true Genoa pesto usually specifies equal quantities of Sardo Pecorino and Parmesan cheeses. Romano Pecorino, which is easily available in this country, is a much sharper cheese than Parmesan. Increasing the proportion of Parmesan to the Romano Pecorino achieves a better balance of flavor.

Combine the basil, garlic, cheeses, and nuts in a food processor or blender. Process to mix. With the machine running, slowly add the olive oil. Season to taste with salt and freshly ground pepper and process to the desired consistency. Let stand 5 minutes before serving.

Yield: About 1 cup

Red Basil Pesto

1-1/2 to 2 cups fresh opal basil
   leaves
2-1/2 tablespoons minced sun-dried
   tomatoes (4 or 5 tomatoes)
2 medium-size garlic cloves
2 tablespoons freshly grated
   Pecorino Romano cheese
6 tablespoons freshly grated
   Parmesan cheese
1/3 cup pine nuts
1/2 cup olive oil
Salt and freshly ground pepper

The addition of sun-dried tomatoes to opal basil produces a pungent, intense pesto that is splendid as a sauce for pasta, fish, and fresh green beans. Sun-dried tomatoes imported from Italy are preserved with herbs and are particularly potent in this extraordinary blend. You'll find a recipe for making your own sun-dried tomatoes on page 126.

Combine the opal basil, sun-dried tomatoes, garlic, cheeses, and pine nuts in a food processor or blender. Process to mix. With the machine running, slowly add the olive oil. Season to taste with salt and freshly ground pepper and process to the desired consistency. Let stand 5 minutes before serving.

Yield: About 1-1/4 cups

Basil and Oregano Pesto

2 cups fresh basil leaves
3 tablespoons fresh oregano leaves
2 medium-size garlic cloves
1/4 cup freshly grated Parmesan
   cheese
1/4 cup walnuts
1/2 cup olive oil
Salt and freshly ground pepper

Basil and oregano combined make an interesting seasoning agent for summer vegetables, soups, and sautéed dishes. Add a little cream and Parmesan cheese to the pesto and toss with hot pasta. Or add a little lemon juice and olive oil to dress a Greek salad.

Combine the basil, oregano, garlic, cheese, and walnuts in a food processor or blender. Process to mix. With the machine running, slowly add the olive oil. Season to taste with salt and freshly ground pepper and process to the desired consistency. Let stand 5 minutes before serving.

Yield: About 1 cup

Basil Mint Pesto

1 cup fresh mint leaves
1 cup fresh basil leaves
2 medium-size garlic cloves
1/4 cup freshly grated Parmesan
  cheese
1/4 cup pine nuts or walnuts
1/2 cup olive oil
· Salt and freshly ground pepper

A fresh sharp flavor. Freeze some to serve on the side with hearty winter soups. Or stuff mushrooms with Basil Mint Pesto and top with a few bread crumbs.

Combine the mint, basil, garlic, cheese, and nuts in a food processor or blender. Process to mix. With the motor running, slowly add the olive oil. Season to taste with salt and freshly ground pepper and process to the desired consistency. Let stand 5 minutes before serving.

Yield: About 1 cup

Sorrel Basil Pesto

2 cups roughly chopped fresh sorrel
    leaves, stem and center vein
    removed
1 cup fresh basil leaves
1 large garlic clove
3 tablespoons freshly grated
    Parmesan cheese
1/4 cup pine nuts
1/3 cup olive oil
Salt and freshly ground pepper

Sorrel grows easily in the garden, and the lemony, juicy leaves make a refreshing, light, piquant pesto with a nice green color. Serve the pesto over fresh pasta or with poached salmon or mussels. It makes a delightful soup with the addition of zucchini and chicken broth (page 79).

Combine the sorrel, basil, garlic, cheese, and pine nuts in a food processor or blender. Process to mix. With the machine running, slowly add the olive oil. Season to taste with salt and freshly ground pepper and process to the desired consistency. Let stand 5 minutes before serving.

Yield: About 1 cup

Watercress and Basil Pesto

1 cup fresh basil leaves
1 cup fresh watercress leaves, stems
   removed
2 medium-size garlic cloves
3 tablespoons freshly grated
   Parmesan cheese
1/4 cup pine nuts
1/3 cup plus 1 tablespoon olive oil
Salt and freshly ground pepper

A mild pesto with a lovely bright green color. Add a little cream and toss with pasta, or serve on poached fish and boiled new potatoes for a delicate treat.

Combine the basil, watercress, garlic, cheese, and nuts in a food processor or blender. Process to mix. With the machine running, slowly add the olive oil. Season to taste with salt and freshly ground pepper and process to the desired consistency. Let stand 5 minutes before serving.

Yield: About 1 cup

Creamy Basil Pesto

2 cups fresh basil leaves
2 large garlic cloves
1/2 cup freshly grated Parmesan
   cheese
3 tablespoons fresh whole milk
   ricotta cheese
1/2 cup walnuts
1/2 cup olive oil
Salt and freshly ground pepper

Combine the basil, garlic, Parmesan, ricotta, and walnuts in a food processor or blender. Process to mix. With the machine running, slowly add the olive oil. Season to taste with salt and freshly ground pepper and process to the desired consistency. Let stand 5 minutes before serving.

Yield: About 1-1/4 cups

Pistachio Pesto

2 cups fresh basil leaves
2 large garlic cloves
1/4 cup freshly grated Parmesan
cheese
1/3 cup shelled unsalted pistachio
nuts
1/2 cup olive oil
Salt and freshly ground pepper

Pistachio pesto is an interesting variation on the Classic Basil Pesto and can be used interchangeably in recipes. The pistachios add a subtle, pleasant flavor of their own. Serve it over pasta or use in any recipe specifying a basil pesto.

Combine the basil, garlic, cheese, and pistachio nuts in a food processor or blender. Process to mix. With the machine running, slowly add the olive oil. Season to taste with salt and freshly ground pepper and process to the desired consistency. Let stand 5 minutes before serving.

Yield: About 1-1/4 cups

Cilantro Pesto

1-1/2 cups fresh cilantro leaves, or
   1 cup fresh cilantro leaves and
   1/2 cup fresh parsley leaves
1 large garlic clove
1/4 cup freshly grated Parmesan
   cheese
3 tablespoons pine nuts
1 teaspoon grated lime peel
5 tablespoons olive oil
Salt and freshly ground pepper

Cilantro, also known as fresh coriander, and Chinese parsley, makes a distinctive subtle pesto with (some claim) an addictive flavor. It makes an excellent pasta sauce. Combine with butter and serve with green beans, summer squash, zucchini, or corn-on-the-cob (page 101). Use it to make dips, salad dressings, and sauces for seafood.

Combine the cilantro, garlic, cheese, pine nuts, and lime peel in a food processor or blender. Process to mix. With the machine running, slowly add the olive oil. Season to taste with salt and freshly ground pepper and process to the desired consistency. Let stand for at least 5 minutes before serving.

Yield: About 2/3 cup

Fennel Pesto

2 tablespoons fennel seeds
1 cup hot water
2 cups roughly chopped fennel
    root, white bulbous part only
    (about 1 large bulb)
1 cup fresh parsley leaves
2 medium-size garlic cloves
1/4 cup freshly grated Parmesan
    cheese
1/4 cup walnuts
1/2 cup olive oil
Salt and freshly ground pepper

Fennel gives this light green pesto a pleasant anise flavor. Add a little cream and sliced roasted red peppers to make a delightful pasta sauce.

Cover the fennel seed with hot water and set aside while you prepare the fennel root.

Steam the roughly chopped fennel root until softened slightly, 4 to 5 minutes. Transfer to a food processor or blender. Drain the fennel seeds. Add the fennel seeds, parsley, garlic, cheese, and walnuts to the fennel root. Process to mix. With the machine running, slowly add the olive oil. Season to taste with salt and freshly ground pepper and process to the desired consistency. Let stand for at least 5 minutes before serving.

Yield: About 1-1/2 cups

Garlic Chive Pesto

1/2 cup roughly chopped fresh
    garlic chives
1 cup fresh parsley leaves
3 tablespoons freshly grated
    Parmesan cheese
1 small garlic clove
3 tablespoons walnuts
5 to 6 tablespoons olive oil
Salt and freshly ground pepper

Make this pesto in the spring when the chives are young. Regular hollow-stemmed chives should not be substituted for flat-bladed garlic chives.

Combine the garlic chives, parsley, cheese, garlic, and walnuts in a food processor or blender. Process to mix. With the machine running, slowly add the olive oil. Season to taste with salt and freshly ground pepper and process to the desired consistency. Let stand for at least 5 minutes before serving.

If you do not plan to use all the Garlic Chive Pesto at once, freeze the extra in small containers to retain its flavor.

Yield: About 2/3 cup

Mediterranean Pesto

2 large garlic cloves
2 tablespoons fresh rosemary leaves
1 tablespoon fresh thyme leaves
1 tablespoon fresh summer savory
   leaves
1 tablespoon fresh oregano leaves
1 cup fresh parsley leaves
1/3 cup freshly ground Parmesan
   cheese
1/2 cup walnuts
1/3 cup plus 1 tablespoon olive oil
Salt and freshly ground pepper

Both the winter and summer versions of this pesto are favorites of mine. Add this pesto to soups, fish stews and sautéed vegetables. Baste lamb or chicken with the pesto thinned with basting juices and a little oil or wine. Or try adding a few table-spoons of the pesto to a bread recipe for an aromatic herb bread (page 96).

Combine the garlic, rosemary, thyme, summer savory, oregano, parsley, cheese, and walnuts in a food processor or blender. Process to mix. With the motor running, slowly add the olive oil. Season to taste with salt and freshly ground pepper and process to the desired consistency. Let stand 5 minutes before serving.

Yield: About 3/4 cup

Oregano Pesto

1/2 cup fresh oregano leaves
1-1/2 cups fresh parsley leaves
2 large garlic cloves
1/2 cup freshly grated Parmesan
   cheese
1/2 cup walnuts or pine nuts
1/2 cup olive oil
Salt and freshly ground pepper

A nice summer pesto, delicious with tomatoes, zucchini, and eggplant. Add a little cream and Parmesan cheese and toss with fresh pasta.

The pesto will be more flavorful if you use a good culinary variety of oregano. The low-growing Greek oregano and the higher-growing Italian oregano are the most flavorful varieties.

Combine the oregano, parsley, garlic, cheese, and nuts in a food processor or blender. Process to mix. With the machine running, slowly add the olive oil. Season to taste and process to the desired consistency. Let stand 5 minutes before serving.

Yield: About 1-1/4 cups

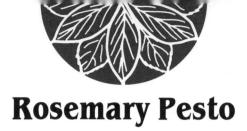

Rosemary Pesto

1/3 cup fresh rosemary leaves
1-1/2 cups fresh parsley leaves
2 large garlic cloves
1/2 cup freshly grated Parmesan
    cheese
1/2 cup walnuts
1/2 cup olive oil
Salt and freshly ground pepper

An intense, aromatic pesto. Use this pesto as a sauce or marinade base for vegetables, seafood, and lamb.

Combine the rosemary, parsley, garlic, cheese, and walnuts in a food processor or blender. Process to mix. With the machine running, slowly add the olive oil. Season to taste with salt and freshly ground pepper and process to the desired consistency. Let stand 5 minutes before serving.

Yield: About 1 cup

Sage Pesto

1/2 cup fresh sage leaves
1-1/2 cups fresh parsley leaves
2 large garlic cloves
1/2 cup freshly grated Parmesan
   cheese
1/2 cup pine nuts or walnuts
1/2 cup olive oil
Salt and freshly ground pepper

The rich flavors of Sage Pesto, cream, and shitake mushrooms make a delicious sauce (page 46) for pasta or spaetzle. Try Sage Pesto under the skin of chicken breasts or with pine nuts and fresh bread crumbs stuffed into Cornish game hens.

Combine the sage, parsley, garlic, cheese, and nuts in a food processor or blender. Process to mix. With the machine running, slowly add the olive oil. Season to taste with salt and freshly ground pepper and process to the desired consistency. Let stand 5 minutes before serving.

Yield: About 1 cup

Savory Pesto

1/2 cup fresh savory leaves
1-1/2 cups fresh parsley leaves
2 large garlic cloves
1/2 cup freshly grated Parmesan
   cheese
1/2 cup walnuts or pine nuts
1/2 cup olive oil
Salt and freshly ground pepper

Add a little cream to the pesto and toss with chopped parsley and freshly cooked linguine. Sauté vegetables with this pesto to use as a filling for warm pita bread or omelets.

Combine the savory, parsley, garlic, cheese, and nuts in a food processor or blender. Process to mix. With the machine running, slowly add the olive oil. Season to taste with salt and freshly ground pepper and process to the desired consistency. Let stand 5 minutes before serving.

Yield: About 1-1/4 cups

Sorrel Pesto with Lemon

2 cups roughly chopped fresh sorrel
    leaves, stem and center vein
    removed
1 cup fresh basil leaves
1 medium-size garlic clove
1 tablespoon fresh lemon juice
3 to 4 tablespoons pine nuts
6 tablespoons olive oil
Salt and freshly ground pepper

Serve Sorrel Pesto with steamed mussels and poached salmon. Fill a hollowed-out artichoke with this green sauce and serve it as a dip with crudités.

Combine the sorrel, basil, garlic, lemon juice, and pine nuts in a food processor or blender. Process to mix. With the machine running, slowly add the olive oil. Season generously with salt and freshly ground pepper and process until smooth. Let stand 5 minutes before serving.

Yield: About 1 cup

Tarragon Pesto

1/2 cup fresh tarragon leaves
1-1/2 cups fresh parsley leaves
2 large garlic cloves
Scant 1/2 cup freshly grated
   Parmesan cheese
1/2 cup pine nuts
1/2 cup olive oil
Salt and freshly ground pepper

Tarragon makes an aromatic, versatile pesto. You can add a little cream to it and serve the sauce over fresh pasta. Or use the pesto as a base for fish sauces and salad dressings. Tuck some Tarragon Pesto under the skin of chicken breasts and bake them, or make a tarragon dressing for a chicken salad (page 92). French tarragon is far more flavorful than other varieties.

Combine the tarragon, parsley, garlic, cheese, and pine nuts in a food processor or blender. Process to mix. With the machine running, slowly add the olive oil. Season to taste with salt and freshly ground pepper and process to the desired consistency. Let stand 5 minutes before serving.

Yield: About 1-1/4 cups

Creamy Tarragon Pesto

1 cup fresh tarragon leaves
1/2 cup fresh parsley leaves
1 large garlic clove
1/3 cup freshly grated Parmesan
  cheese
1/2 cup walnuts
2 tablespoons whipping cream
1 tablespoon hot water
1/2 cup olive oil
About 2 tablespoons lemon juice
Salt and freshly ground pepper

This is a creamy light pesto of fresh tarragon, lemon, and walnuts. It is especially nice with angel hair pasta and delicate seafood dishes, such as trout and smoked eel.

Combine the tarragon, parsley, garlic, cheese, walnuts, cream, and water in a food processor or blender. Process to mix. With the machine running, slowly add the olive oil. Add the lemon juice, salt, and freshly ground pepper to taste. Process to the desired consistency. Let stand 5 minutes before serving.

Yield: About 1 cup

Thyme Pesto

1/2 cup fresh thyme leaves
1-1/2 cups fresh parsley leaves
2 large garlic cloves
1/2 cup freshly grated Parmesan
    cheese
1/2 cup pine nuts or walnuts
1/2 cup olive oil
Salt and freshly ground pepper

Stripping the small thyme leaves from the stem is a time-consuming task, but well worth the effort for this pungent pesto. Serve over pasta with grilled summer vegetables—red and yellow peppers, Japanese eggplants, and plum tomatoes—or with fresh seafood and scallops.

Combine the thyme, parsley, garlic, cheese, and nuts in a food processor or blender. Process to mix. With the machine running, slowly add the olive oil. Season to taste with salt and freshly ground pepper and process to the desired consistency. Let stand 5 minutes before serving.

Yield: About 1-1/4 cups

Caraway Thyme Pesto

1/2 cup fresh caraway thyme leaves
1 cup fresh parsley leaves
2 medium-size garlic cloves
1/3 cup freshly grated Parmesan
   cheese
1/2 cup walnuts
1/2 cup olive oil
Salt and freshly ground pepper

Caraway thyme has a strong aromatic flavor reminiscent of both caraway and thyme. It is one of the more exciting of the culinary herbs and makes an excellent pesto. Combine the pesto with butter to make a sauce with fresh vegetables, or use it as a basting ingredient with seafood.

Combine the caraway thyme, parsley, garlic, cheese, and walnuts in a food processor or blender. Process to mix. With the machine running, slowly add the olive oil. Season to taste with salt and freshly ground pepper and process to the desired consistency. Let stand for at least 5 minutes before serving.

Yield: About 3/4 cup

Oregano Thyme Pesto

1/2 cup fresh oregano thyme leaves
1 cup fresh parsley leaves
2 medium-size garlic cloves
1/3 cup freshly grated Parmesan
   cheese
1/2 cup walnuts
1/2 cup olive oil
Salt and freshly ground pepper

Here's another lesser known culinary thyme well worth cultivating for pestos—oregano thyme. Like caraway thyme, it has a pungent flavor that is quite aromatic and distinctive.

Combine the oregano thyme, parsley, garlic, cheese, and walnuts in a food processor or blender. Process to mix. With the machine running, slowly add the olive oil. Season to taste with salt and freshly ground pepper and process to the desired consistency. Let stand 5 minutes before serving.

Yield: About 3/4 cup

Garlic Thyme Pesto

1/2 cup garlic cloves, peeled (giant
  garlic is easier)
1/2 cup olive oil
2 tablespoons fresh or dried thyme
1/4 cup walnuts
2 tablespoons freshly grated
  Parmesan cheese
Approximately 3/4 cup spinach
  leaves, carefully washed
1/4 teaspoon salt or to taste
Freshly ground pepper

A base of garlic confit gives an interesting sweet flavor to this winter or summer pesto. Excellent as a base for a pasta sauce or to flavor a calzone or omelet filling.

Simmer the whole peeled garlic cloves in olive oil in a small saucepan at the lowest possible heat for about 20 minutes. Do not brown! Cool the garlic cloves in the oil.

Combine the ingredients in a blender and blend to a smooth paste, scraping down the sides of the blender as needed. Add the spinach leaves and blend to the consistency desired. Taste for salt and pepper. Herbs vary in strength. You may wish to add more thyme. Let stand for at least 5 minutes before serving.

Yield: 2/3 cup

Winter Mixed Herb Pesto

1 cup fresh parsley leaves
1 tablespoon dried sage
1 teaspoon dried thyme
1-1/2 teaspoons dried marjoram
2 medium-size garlic cloves
3 tablespoons freshly grated
  Parmesan cheese
1/4 cup walnuts
6 tablespoons olive oil
Salt and freshly ground pepper

This sage, thyme, and marjoram mix makes a pungent pesto. It can be made in the winter—all year round, in fact—because it is made with dried herbs. Use it in a calzone filling (page 119), with mushrooms in an omelet, or to season sautéed vegetables.

Combine the parsley, sage, thyme, marjoram, garlic, cheese, and walnuts in a blender. Process to mix. With the machine running, slowly add the olive oil. Season to taste with salt and pepper and process to the desired consistency. Let stand 5 minutes before serving.

Yield: About 3/4 cup

Winter Mediterranean Pesto

2 large garlic cloves
2 teaspoons dried rosemary
1-1/2 teaspoons dried thyme
1 teaspoon dried summer savory
1 teaspoon dried oregano
1 cup fresh parsley leaves
1/3 cup freshly grated Parmesan
  cheese
1/2 cup pine nuts or walnuts
1/3 cup plus 1 tablespoon olive oil
Salt and freshly ground pepper

This pesto has a strong heady aroma and is delicious in soups and dishes with a tomato base. It brings forth the flavors of sautéed vegetables very nicely. Added to the juices of chicken or lamb, it makes a delightful basting sauce.

Combine the garlic, rosemary, thyme, summer savory, oregano, parsley, cheese, and nuts in a blender. Process to mix. With the blender running, slowly add the olive oil. Season to taste with salt and freshly ground pepper and process to the desired consistency. Let stand for 5 minutes before serving.

Yield: About 3/4 cup

Winter Thyme Pesto

1 cup fresh parsley leaves
2 tablespoons dried thyme
2 medium-size garlic cloves
3 tablespoons freshly grated
   Parmesan cheese
1/4 cup walnuts
6 tablespoons olive oil
Salt and freshly ground pepper

Thyme makes a pungent pesto that is great to have on hand for soups and sauces, or to use as a basting ingredient. I like to sauté vegetables, seafood, and rice pilaf in butter mixed with Winter Thyme Pesto.

Combine the parsley, thyme, garlic, cheese, and walnuts in a blender. Process to mix. With the blender running, slowly add the olive oil. Season to taste with salt and freshly ground pepper and process to the desired consistency. Let stand 5 minutes before serving.

Yield: About 3/4 cup

Winter Lemon Thyme Pesto

3 strips of lemon peel, no white
   pith (about 1-1/2 teaspoons)
3/4 cup fresh parsley leaves
2 tablespoons dried thyme
2 medium-size garlic cloves
2 tablespoons lemon juice
1/4 cup pine nuts
6 tablespoons olive oil
Salt and freshly ground pepper

The lemony thyme flavor of this pesto is nicely assertive with seafood. I use this pesto in Bay Scallops with Lemon Thyme Crumbs (page 104), but this pesto is equally delicious used as a basting ingredient. Combined with a little butter, it makes a delicious sauce for vegetables.

Dried thyme may include woody stems. Purchase or gather stem-free thyme or pick through the leaves carefully to remove the stems.

Combine the lemon peel, parsley, thyme, garlic, lemon juice, and pine nuts in a blender. Process to mix. With the blender running, add the olive oil. Season to taste with salt and freshly ground pepper and process to the desired consistency. Let stand 5 minutes before serving.

Yield: About 1 cup

VARIATION
  Substitute freshly grated Parmesan cheese to taste in place of the lemon juice.

Winter Kale Pesto

1 cup chopped fresh kale, stems
   removed
1/2 cup dried basil
2 medium-size garlic cloves
2 tablespoons freshly grated
   Parmesan cheese
1/4 cup sunflower seeds
3/4 cup olive oil
Salt and freshly ground pepper

Kale and sunflower seeds make up this unusual dark green winter pesto. Toss with a firm-textured whole wheat pasta and Parmesan cheese or try it with Linguine and Broccoli (page 59).

Combine the kale, basil, garlic, cheese, and sunflower seeds in a blender. Process to mix. With the blender running, slowly add the olive oil. Season to taste with salt and freshly ground pepper and process to the desired consistency.

Yield: About 1-1/4 cups

Winter Mint Pesto

2 tablespoons dried mint leaves
1 cup fresh parsley leaves
2 tablespoons freshly grated
    Parmesan cheese
2 medium-size garlic cloves
3 tablespoons pine nuts or walnuts
6 tablespoons olive oil
Salt and freshly ground pepper

This one is a surprise: a pesto with mint has a sharp pleasurable zing. It is altogether wonderful in minestrone; I add a dollop to each bowl at the last moment.

Combine the mint, parsley, cheese, garlic, and nuts in a food processor or blender. Process to mix. With the machine running, slowly add the olive oil. Season to taste with salt and freshly ground pepper and process to the desired consistency. Let stand 5 minutes before serving.

Yield: About 3/4 cup

Anchovy Herb Pesto

1 to 1-1/2 tablespoons anchovy
    paste or chopped anchovy fillets
1 cup fresh parsley leaves
1 tablespoon dried oregano
1 tablespoon dried thyme
2 medium-size garlic cloves
1/4 cup freshly grated Parmesan
    cheese
1/4 cup walnuts
1/3 cup olive oil
Freshly ground pepper

With the addition of a little lemon juice or vinegar, this winter pesto makes an excellent dressing for salads and new potatoes (page 90). The strong, rich flavor is delicious with summer vegetables. Try combining this pesto with diced ripe tomatoes and Parmesan cheese and tossing with freshly cooked pasta.

Combine the anchovy paste, parsley, oregano, thyme, garlic, cheese, and walnuts in a food processor or blender. Process to mix. With the machine running, slowly add the olive oil. Season to taste with freshly ground pepper. Process to the desired consistency. Let stand 5 minutes before serving.

Yield: About 3/4 cup

2.
Pasta and Pestos

Pesto and pasta are a natural combination. Pasta/pesto combinations are so simple to prepare and so soothingly satisfying that they are perfect for quick family dining. Yet, these same pasta dishes can be served confidently to the most sophisticated diners at the most elegant parties. With pesto in the refrigerator or freezer and a good pasta on hand, you are prepared for just about anything.

Making Pesto Sauces

It is very simple to make a quick pasta sauce from pesto, and all of the pestos in Chapter 1 taste delicious with pasta. Just bring the pesto to room temperature. Plan to use 2 or 3 tablespoons of pesto for each 4-ounce serving of cooked pasta.

While the pasta cooks, thin the pesto with a few tablespoons of the pasta cooking water. Then toss the hot pasta with the thinned pesto and serve it in a heated dish. Instead of the hot pasta water, you may wish to add 2 or 3 tablespoons of soft butter to the pesto to make an even richer sauce. Many pesto lovers prefer to add a few tablespoons of heavy cream to the pesto before tossing with the pasta.

If you do add cream to the pesto, you may wish to heat the pesto just a little. Don't overheat or you will lose some color and flavor. Heat the pesto in a double boiler, and never allow the pesto to come to a boil. Then toss the warmed pesto with the hot pasta and serve in a heated dish.

Fresh Parmesan cheese should be served at the table with pasta made with the Classic Basil Pesto (page 7), but not with the more delicate pestos, such as Tarragon Pesto (page 24). A good peppermill on the table is a must.

Using pesto as a base, it is easy to invent new sauces. Is there something fresh and wonderful at the store—or in your garden—that can be added to the pesto? Are there small bits and pieces of meat or fish in your refrigerator that will add a flavor accent? Perhaps some finely chopped sautéed red peppers, young shelled fava beans, mushrooms, or broccoli could be added. Pieces of ripe cherry tomato, a little ricotta cheese, steamed mussels, or smoked fish are possibilities for improvisation.

About Pasta

Pasta is found in nearly all countries of the world, in a multitude of shapes and sizes. It's a challenge to identify them all. The Italian cuisine actually is made up of a number of regional cuisines, and each has its own name for the various pasta forms. Manufacturers have added new twists to the names. In addition to the Italian pastas, there are Chinese egg noodles, buckwheat noodles, and spaetzle—all delicious with pesto.

The pasta shapes listed here are some of my favorites, and they all work especially well with pestos.

Angel hair	Very fine, thin long pasta
Taglierini	Narrow flat noodles, about 1/16 inch wide
Spaghetti	Round long pasta, about 1/16 inch wide
Linguine	Narrow flat noodles, about 1/8 inch wide
Tagliatelle	Narrow flat noodles, about 1/4 inch wide
Fettuccine	Narrow flat noodles, about 5/8 inch wide
Fusilli	Corkscrew shape, long or short noodles
Orzo	Rice-shaped pasta, about 3/8-1/2 inch long
Small shells	Shell-shaped pasta, about 1/2-3/4 inch wide
Farfalle	Bow-shaped pasta, about 3/4 inch long
Tubetti	Narrow short tubes, about 3/4 inch long
Penne	Large short tubes, about 1 inch long
Tortellini	Small curled filled pasta, about 1 inch long
Ravioli	Square filled pasta, about 1 inch square
Spaetzle	Small dumpling bits, about 1/2 inch long

Cooking Pasta

The only rule for cooking pasta is that you need a big pot with plenty of boiling water so that the pasta can boil furiously. Since the time it takes to cook will vary with the pasta, you must test it for doneness at very frequent intervals.

A fresh pasta may be cooked *al dente* (tender to the bite) in 2 to 3 minutes, but a dried pasta may take 4 to 6 minutes if made with an all-purpose flour. A durum wheat pasta in a large shape will take anywhere from 8 to 15 minutes to cook to tenderness. The only successful way to cook pasta is to taste the strands continually, until the "just tender" stage is reached.

A long wooden spoon is helpful to stir and separate the pasta strands because it does not tear the pasta or conduct heat. When the pasta is ready, it can be lifted out of the water with tongs, a wooden pegged pasta fork, or a large Oriental wire-mesh spoon. Or you can drain the pasta in a large colander. Either return the pasta to the warm pot briefly while you ready the sauce, or place it in a heated bowl. Do not let it sit in the colander or it will become a gluey mass. If the pasta does become gluey, rinse it in very hot water.

Plan to serve the pasta immediately or toss it hot with some or all of the sauce. If you are cooking the pasta for a salad, add a little oil and toss it gently to keep the strands separate as they cool.

The number of servings per pound of pasta depend on the appetites of the diners and the place of the pasta in the meal. Generally, a pound of pasta should make 6 to 8 first course servings and 4 to 6 main course servings.

During recent years fresh pasta shops have opened in most cities, and they frequently market their products in the supermarkets. Fresh store-bought pasta is best used within a few days or frozen for a couple of weeks. Longer than that, the pasta will dry and lose flavor. I use a good dry commercial product as often as a purchased fresh pasta. Frequently the quality is superior. The advantages of a good quality dry commercial pasta made with durum wheat is that it keeps well, is inexpensive, has a uniform assured quality, and is made in a large variety of shapes.

Making Pasta at Home

Making pasta at home is a real treat. But even with the help of machines, it does take time to prepare the surfaces for making pasta and to get out the machines, ingredients, drying rack, and so on. Making good pasta is a serious art.

The best flour to use for pasta is hard wheat flour, called durum wheat flour. It has more gluten than all-purpose flour and is easier to knead and roll out. But the recipes will work with all-purpose flour, although you may have to add extra flour or oil for the right consistency, particularly if the dough is mixed by machine. Durum wheat flour often can be found in health food stores and some supermarkets and specialty food stores.

The quality of the eggs you use will make a difference in your pasta. If you can get fresh eggs from local free-ranging chickens that are not fed steroids and antibiotics, you will have a far superior golden pasta with real flavor. It is worth finding a good source for eggs if you plan to make pasta frequently.

Hand-cut noodles or a simple fettuccine or linguine can be made fairly easily and quickly. Made with quality ingredients, they provide a perfect vehicle for a wonderful homemade pesto.

Basic Egg Pasta

2 cups durum wheat flour (or
    unbleached all-purpose flour)
1/2 teaspoon salt
3 large eggs
2 teaspoons olive oil
Small amount of water, if necessary
    (about 1 teaspoon)

Mixing the Dough in a Food Processor

To make the dough in a food processor, combine the flour and salt in the processor fitted with a steel blade. With the machine running, add the eggs and olive oil through the feed tube. Process for about 15 seconds. Remove the cover and squeeze pieces of dough. Add a little water if the dough feels too dry. Add 1 to 2 tablespoons flour, if the dough is sticky. Process briefly.

Turn the dough out onto a floured board. Knead for 1 to 2 minutes (the food processor already has kneaded it somewhat). Place the dough ball in a plastic bag.

If you are using a pasta machine, proceed with the rolling. If you are rolling by hand, let the dough ball rest at room temperature for 15 to 30 minutes, or longer. (You can hold it in the refrigerator for up to 2 or 3 days.)

Mixing the Dough by Hand

To mix the dough by hand, place the flour and salt in a bowl. Beat the eggs and oil together. Make a well in the center of the flour and add the beaten eggs and oil. With a fork, combine the flour into the eggs. When it is all mixed, add a little water only if the dough seems dry.

Turn the dough out onto a floured board. Knead until a smooth elastic ball is formed, about 5 to 10 minutes. Push the dough with the heels of your hands, folding and turning until you have a smooth dough. Place the dough ball in a plastic bag or cover with a dish towel. Let rest at room temperature for 15 to 30 minutes.

Rolling the Dough by Machine

To roll by machine, set the rollers at the thickest setting. Divide the dough into 4 balls. Take 1 dough ball and flatten it with your palms. Flour the dough lightly. Run the dough through the rollers 3 or 4 times. Cut the dough to the desired pasta length. Set the rollers at a middle setting on the dial. Run through again 3 or 4 times. Roll again at a thinner setting, depending on the thickness you wish to achieve. Fit the cutting attachment in place. Insert the handle if you are using a hand-cranked model. Proceed to feed the dough into the machine, catching the pasta strands with your arm as they are rolled from the machine.

Rolling the Dough by Hand

To roll by hand, press the dough out to a circle on a floured board. Roll from the center out, giving the dough a quarter turn each time you roll. Be sure the dough does not stick to the board. If it does stick, loosen it from the board and add flour. Continue rolling and stretching the dough until you have reached the thinness you desire. Let the dough rest a few minutes under kitchen towels to dry a little. Either slice the pasta to width by hand, or roll the dough loosely into a flat 3-inch-wide roll and cut slices from the rolled dough. Toss the pasta lightly in a little flour and cornmeal.

If you do not plan to cook the pasta immediately, it can be stored in a tightly sealed container in the refrigerator for 2 or 3 days. Or dry the pasta, uncovered, for 3 or 4 hours at room temperature and store in plastic bags for a few days or in the freezer for 2 or 3 weeks.

Yield: 4 servings

Artichoke and Mushroom Pasta Sauce

2 tablespoons butter
1/4 cup diced shallots
3 baby artichokes, quartered, or
    one 10-ounce package frozen
    artichoke hearts, thawed and
    halved lengthwise
2 tablespoons Tarragon Pesto (page
    24)
2 tablespoons any basil pesto (pages
    7-14)
1-3/4 cups sliced mushrooms
2/3 cup heavy cream
Salt and freshly ground pepper

Heat the butter in a large sauté pan and add the shallots. Sauté briefly, about 2 minutes. Add the artichokes and continue to sauté for 3 or 4 minutes, stirring frequently.

Stir in the pestos and the mushrooms. Add the cream, and simmer until the artichokes and mushrooms are tender and the liquid is reduced by a third, about 6 to 8 minutes, stirring very little. Taste, and adjust for seasoning—adding, perhaps more pesto, or salt and pepper.

Serve over hot angel hair pasta with freshly grated Parmesan cheese.

Yield: About 2 servings

VARIATION
Substitute 1/4 cup Tarragon Pesto for the combination of half Tarragon Pesto and half basil pesto.

Fresh Shitake and Sage Pasta Sauce

3 tablespoons butter
1/2 cup thinly sliced shallots
About 1/4 pound fresh shitake
   mushrooms, julienne sliced in
   thin strips (about 1-1/2 cups)
Salt and freshly ground pepper
1/4 cup chicken broth
1-1/2 cups heavy cream
1 tablespoon Sage Pesto (page 21)
1/4 to 1/2 teaspoon lemon juice

VARIATION
   Fresh wild mushrooms, such as morels, chanterelles, or cèpes (*Boletus edulis*), can be used, although they are not as widely available as the shitakes. Dried shitakes can be substituted. Soak the dried mushrooms in hot water for 30 minutes before proceeding with the recipe.

Fresh shitakes are superior in flavor to dried shitakes. If refrigerated in plastic bags, they will keep for days. Serve this sauce over hot fettuccine and garnish with sage leaves.

In a large skillet, melt the butter, sauté the shallots in the butter very slowly for about 10 minutes. Do not let them brown. Add the shitakes, salt, and pepper and continue sautéing, stirring frequently. Add the chicken broth, a little at a time, as you sauté.

Pour in the cream and simmer very slowly until the sauce is reduced by half (about 15 to 20 minutes), stirring frequently. Add the Sage Pesto and a small amount of lemon juice to taste. Serve hot.

Yield: 4 servings

Fresh Pea and Mint Pesto Pasta Sauce

3/4 pound fresh snow peas or
    young (immature) sugar snap
    peas
2 tablespoons butter
About 3 tablespoons Winter Mint
    Pesto (page 35) or Basil Mint
    Pesto (page 10)
1 cup thinly sliced scallions
1 pint medium cream
Salt and freshly ground pepper

The success of this sauce depends on young, freshly picked peas to give the dish its sweet flavor.

Wash and string the peas. Cut on the diagonal into 1/2-inch slices. You should have about 3 cups.

Melt the butter with 2 tablespoons of the pesto. Add the peas and scallions and sauté over a low heat until tender, 8 to 10 minutes. Add the cream, and salt and pepper to taste. Reduce until the sauce is slightly thickened, about 2 minutes. Stir in the remaining 1 tablespoon of the pesto. Taste and adjust for seasoning. Toss with hot pasta and serve.

Yield: 4 servings

Carrot and Summer Savory Sauce

3-4 tablespoons butter
1 1/2 cups finely diced baby carrots
2/3 cups finely diced shallots
1 1/3 cups finely diced ripe
tomatoes, drained (ripe cherry
tomatoes or plum tomatoes work
well here)
4-6 tablespoons Savory Pesto (page 22)
About 1/2 cup whipping cream
Salt and freshly ground pepper
1/4 teaspoon lemon juice or to
taste

Melt the butter in a large sauté pan, and sauté the carrots slowly for 2 or 3 minutes, being careful not to brown them. Add the shallots and continue sautéing for 2 minutes. Add the tomatoes and sauté briefly.

With a fork, gently stir in the pesto, leaving small green pieces. Pour the cream over the vegetables. Season with salt and pepper.

Simmer very briefly, for 1 to 2 minutes, to evaporate some liquid. Stir the sauce as little as possible to retain the texture of the tomatoes and pesto. Add lemon juice to taste.

To serve pour over hot green vermicelli and garnish with chopped Italian flat parsley.

Yield: 4 servings

Eggplant Pasta Sauce

3/4 pound small, thin-skinned Japanese eggplant (or substitute peeled, larger eggplants, if necessary), cut in 1/2-inch cubes (about 3-1/2 to 4 cups)
Salt
3 tablespoons olive oil
1/4 cup Anchovy Herb Pesto (page 36) or Mediterranean Pesto (page 18)
4 leeks, including some light green stem, cleaned and roughly chopped (about 2 cups)
1 cup Italian crushed tomatoes
Salt and freshly ground pepper

A whole wheat pasta, such as fusilli or small shells, complements this pungent, rich eggplant sauce nicely. The sauce can be made a day ahead for a good meld of flavors. Serve over hot pasta with Parmesan cheese on the side.

Sprinkle the cubed eggplant with salt and let it drain in a colander for 30 minutes. Press out as much moisture as possible and dry in a towel.

Heat the olive oil and pesto in a large sauté pan. Add the eggplant cubes and sauté, stirring frequently, for 3 to 4 minutes. Add the leeks and continue to sauté over low heat. You can add a few tablespoons of water to keep the eggplant from scorching and partially cover the pan. When the leeks start to become tender, add the crushed tomatoes. Cook for 3 to 5 minutes. Taste for seasoning. Serve hot.

Yield: 4 servings

Sweet Red Pepper Sauce

3 tablespoons olive oil
2 cups diced sweet red peppers
1 cup diced onion
3 to 4 tablespoons water
About 3 tablespoons Red Basil
    Pesto (page 8)
2 tablespoons dry white wine
Salt and freshly ground pepper
Pinch cayenne (optional)

This mellow red sauce provides the perfect foil for cape scallops. For a pasta sauce, add shrimp, squid, or chopped tomatoes and toss with hot pasta.

Heat the oil in a large sauté pan and add the peppers and onion. Sauté, stirring frequently, until the peppers and onion begin to soften. Add the water, cover, and simmer for 5 minutes.

Pour the sautéed vegetables into a blender or food processor and blend until smooth. Return the mixture to the pan and bring to a simmer. Blend in the pesto and wine. Season to taste with salt, pepper, and cayenne, if you wish. Serve hot or cold.

Yield: About 1-1/2 cups

Red Pesto and Pepper Sauce

1 tablespoon butter
1 tablespoon olive oil
1 cup julienne-sliced sweet red
   peppers
1 cup julienne-sliced sweet yellow
   peppers
1 cup julienne-sliced sweet "white"
   or green peppers
1/3 cup diced sweet red onion
3 to 4 tablespoons Red Basil Pesto
   (page 8)
1/2 cup chicken broth
Salt and freshly ground pepper

Large sweet red and yellow peppers have appeared more frequently in the markets in recent years. They make a colorful pasta sauce.

Heat the butter and oil in a sauté pan. Add the peppers and sauté, stirring frequently, for about 5 minutes. Add the onion and continue cooking for about 2 minutes. Add the pesto, and chicken broth. Cook until the sauce is reduced by a third. Season to taste with salt and pepper. Serve on hot pasta with freshly grated Parmesan cheese on the side.

Yield: 4 servings (about 2 cups)

VARIATION
   Add sliced zucchini, summer squash, or diced eggplant and sauté with the peppers. Add 1/8 to 1/4 teaspoon dried crushed hot red pepper flakes.

Fresh Tomato Shrimp Pasta Sauce

2 tablespoons olive oil
1 pound small fresh shrimp, peeled
    and deveined (about 2 cups)
1/2 cup minced shallots
2 cups peeled diced tomatoes,
    drained
4 to 6 tablespoons Oregano Thyme
    Pesto (page 28), Thyme Pesto
    (page 26), or Classic Basil Pesto
    (page 7) with 2 teaspoons thyme
    leaves added
2 tablespoons chopped fresh parsley
1/3 to 1/2 cup Crème Fraîche
    (page 124) or heavy cream
Salt and freshly ground pepper
Squeeze of lime or lemon juice

Fresh local shrimp will provide the most flavor for this sauce. Here in the East the small Maine shrimp add a sweet freshness to this dish.

Heat the olive oil in a large sauté pan. Sauté the shrimp and shallots for about 2 minutes. Add the tomatoes and pesto. Simmer for about 3 minutes, until the shrimp are tender and the juices have reduced a little. Do not overcook.

Add the parsley, Crème Fraîche and salt and pepper to taste. Taste the sauce and add a little lemon or lime juice. Serve warm. This sauce is excellent over angel hair pasta.

Yield: 4 servings

Cherry Tomato Pesto Pasta Sauce

3 cups ripe cherry tomatoes
1/4 cup Classic Basil Pesto (page 7)
1/4 cup Thyme Pesto (page 26) or
   Oregano Thyme Pesto (page 28)
1 tablespoon tarragon vinegar
1 tablespoon olive oil
Freshly ground pepper
About 1/2 cup crumbled feta
   cheese
Parmesan cheese

Quarter the cherry tomatoes, removing the stem end as you slice.

Combine the pestos, vinegar, olive oil, and freshly ground pepper. Taste for seasoning. Add the dressing to the tomatoes. Marinate, covered, at room temperature for at least 30 minutes. Or, refrigerate for 3 to 4 hours, then return to room temperature. Serve over hot pasta, with side dishes of feta and Parmesan cheese.

Yield: 4 servings

Green Bean Sage Pesto Pasta Sauce

About 1-1/4 cups fresh bread
crumbs, from light whole wheat
bread (preferably)
About 1-1/2 tablespoons olive oil
2 cups slender fresh green beans,
cut in 1/2-inch dice
4-6 tablespoons Sage Pesto (page
21)
1 tablespoon butter
1/4 cup finely diced sweet yellow or
red peppers
Salt and freshly ground pepper

It is essential to have fresh young green beans in this sauce recipe.

Preheat the oven to 300°F.

Cut the crusts from a good homemade-type bread and cut into chunks. Process briefly in a food processor or crumble into fine crumbs by hand. Spread out the crumbs on a large flat pan and toast in the oven until lightly browned, about 10 minutes. Toss with the olive oil while still hot.

Steam the green beans until barely tender, 5 to 6 minutes. Toss with the pesto and butter while hot. Add the toasted bread crumbs, diced peppers, and salt and pepper to taste. Toss with hot pasta and garnish with fresh sage leaves.

Yield: 4 servings

VARIATION
Finely julienned Italian sun-dried tomatoes (page 126) can be substituted for the sweet peppers. Any basil pesto (pages 7-14) or Savory Pesto (page 22) can be substituted for the Sage Pesto.

Tomato Anchovy Pesto Pasta Sauce

1-1/2 tablespoons butter
1-1/4 to 1-1/2 cups thinly sliced
and quartered Spanish onion
3 tablespoons Anchovy Herb Pesto
(page 36) or to taste
2-1/2 to 3 cups sliced peeled ripe
plum tomatoes
3 to 4 tablespoons thinly sliced salt-
cured dry black olives
Freshly ground pepper

This easy winter or summer pasta sauce combines French Provençal flavors. The salt-cured olives, cultivated along the Mediterranean, are picked fully ripe and cured dry with salt. If fresh ripe tomatoes are unavailable, make the sauce with canned Italian plum tomatoes.

In a large sauté pan, melt the butter. Sauté the onion very slowly for about 10 minutes. The onion should not brown.

Add the pesto, tomatoes, and olive slices. Simmer gently, stirring as little as possible, for about 10 minutes, until the liquids are reduced by a third. Season to taste with freshly ground pepper. Toss with freshly cooked pasta and serve hot.

Yield: 4 servings

Fresh Clam Pasta Sauce

2 pounds very fresh steamer clams
2 tablespoons chopped onion
2 tablespoons roughly chopped
   parsley leaves
1 bay leaf, crumbled
1/4 cup white wine
1/4 cup water
1-1/2 tablespoons butter
1/3 cup finely diced carrot
1/3 cup finely diced onion
1/3 cup finely diced shallots
1 cup or more diced peeled ripe
   tomatoes, drained
1/4 cup clam juice (cooking liquid
   from the clams)
2 tablespoons heavy cream
   (optional)
1 tablespoon Thyme Pesto (page 26)
1 tablespoon Oregano Pesto (page 19)
Chopped parsley
Freshly ground pepper

This sauce takes time to prepare, but the expense is nil and the results are delicious. The clam juice is naturally salty, so add only freshly ground pepper. I like the sauce served over an angel hair tomato herb pasta.

This dish can be partially prepared in advance. Steam the clams and remove the meat. Chop to the desired size and refrigerate covered with some clam broth. Prepare the vegetables and refrigerate. Sauté the vegetables and clams, and cook the pasta just before serving.

Wash and scrub the clams thoroughly. Put them in a large covered pot with the 2 tablespoons chopped onion, 2 tablespoons chopped parsley, the bay leaf, white wine, and water. Steam over high heat just until the clams open. Remove from the pot and set aside to cool a little. Strain the juices into a large measuring cup to allow the sand to settle. Discard any clams that have not opened.

Remove the clams from their shells, removing the tough neck from Eastern littleneck clams. Cover the clam meat with some of the clam broth poured carefully from the top of the measuring cup (leaving any sand on the bottom). Refrigerate the clams.

Heat the butter in a large sauté pan and add the carrot, the remaining 1/3 cup onion, and the shallots. Sauté until barely tender, stirring frequently, for 3 to 5 minutes. Add the tomatoes and 1/4 cup clam juice, and reduce the liquids by half, cooking for about 4 minutes.

Roughly chop the clams to the size of the chopped tomatoes.

Stir the cream and the pestos into the sauté pan with the vegetables. Add the clams, chopped parsley, and freshly ground pepper. Reheat for about 1 minute, but no longer, or the clams will toughen. Taste. You may wish to add more pesto. Immediately serve with hot pasta.

Yield: 2-3 servings

Sausage and Fennel Pesto Pasta Sauce

6 fresh hot Italian sausages (or 3
   sweet and 3 hot sausages)
1 tablespoon olive oil
1-1/2 cups diced onions
4 to 6 tablespoons Fennel Pesto
   (page 16)
1/3 to 1/2 cup light cream
Salt and freshly ground pepper

I like hot Italian sausages in this recipe, but you may prefer a combination of sweet and hot sausage. Serve with fresh linguine, hand-cut noodles, or corkscrew pasta.

Slice the sausage casings open on 1 side and remove the sausage meat. Heat the olive oil in a large sauté pan and sauté the sausage for about 5 minutes, stirring occasionally and crumbling the meat into small pieces.

Drain the oil from the sausage meat, and return the sausage to the pan. Add the onions, cover, and simmer slowly until the sausage is cooked. Add the pesto and cream. Season to taste with salt and freshly ground pepper. Toss with the hot pasta and serve with freshly grated Parmesan cheese at the table.

Yield: 4 servings

VARIATIONS

Add 1 cup sliced fresh fennel with the onion and sauté until tender. Proceed with the recipe.

Add 1 cup peeled, seeded, and diced tomato with the pesto and cream.

Add 1-1/2 cups small fresh cauliflower florets and a few tablespoons of diced sweet red pepper with the onion. Proceed with the recipe.

Linguine with Broccoli and Pesto

4 quarts water
3/4 pound fresh spinach linguine
1 tablespoon salt
3 tablespoons olive oil
1 tablespoon butter
1-1/2 cups finely diced broccoli
    stems
1-1/2 cups small broccoli florets
6 tablespoons pesto (Pistachio
    Pesto, page 14 or Winter Kale
    Pesto, page 34, are rec-
    ommended)
1/3 cup pine nuts
1/3 cup freshly grated Parmesan
    cheese
Salt and freshly ground pepper

Bring the water to a boil in a deep saucepan. Drop the pasta and a tablespoon salt into boiling water and return to a boil. Cook briefly, testing frequently, until the pasta is *al dente* (just tender). Drain well. Toss with 1 tablespoon of the olive oil and set aside.

Heat the remaining 2 tablespoons of olive oil and the butter in a sauté pan, and sauté the diced broccoli stems for about 2 minutes, stirring frequently. Add the broccoli florets and continue stirring and sautéing until the broccoli is barely soft.

Add the pesto and drained linguine to the broccoli in the sauté pan. Stir over a low heat for 2 to 3 minutes. Add the pine nuts, grated cheese, salt, and freshly ground pepper to taste. Serve hot with extra grated Parmesan cheese on the side.

Yield: 4 servings

Rosemary Pesto Confit for Pasta

2 tablespoons butter
2 tablespoons virgin olive oil
3 cups very thinly sliced onions
Salt and freshly ground pepper
1/8 teaspoon sugar
1 to 2 tablespoons full-bodied red
    wine
1/2 pound cob-smoked ham, sliced
    1/2 inch thick
About 1-1/2 tablespoons Rosemary
    Pesto (page 20)
Salt and freshly ground pepper

Confit usually refers to duck or goose cooked slowly in its own fat and preserved in its own fat and juices. The confit method of slow cooking and storing in the juices and oils has been adapted to other foods in recent years. This simplified onion confit and smoky ham with rosemary pesto makes a flavorful combination with pasta. Cooking the onions very slowly and adding a little sugar and red wine as the sauté produces a rich brown glaze, enhancing the natural sweetness of the onions. A quality cob-smoked ham makes all the difference in flavor in this dish.

Heat the butter and 1 tablespoon of the oil in a large sauté pan. Add the onions, salt, and pepper. Sauté very slowly, stirring frequently for 10 minutes. Do not brown. Add the sugar and red wine. Continue sautéing very slowly until the onions are a

little caramelized, about 20 minutes.
Remove the onions from the pan with a
slotted spoon.

The onion confit may be prepared at any
time. It will keep for about a week in the
refrigerator. Use it with vegetables, pasta
dishes, omelets, sandwiches.

To complete this dish, heat the remaining
1 tablespoon oil and sauté the ham over a
high heat until lightly browned. Return the
onions to the pan and heat briefly. Add the
pesto, salt, pepper to taste. Serve over hot
pasta.

Yield: 2 servings

Pesto Pasta with Salmon Cream

1 recipe Basic Egg Pasta (page 12)
3 tablespoons Classic Basil Pesto
  (page 7)
3 tablespoons butter
6 tablespoons thinly sliced shallots
1-1/2 cups heavy cream
Freshly ground pepper
4 quarts water
Salt
4 to 5 tablespoons Red Basil Pesto
  (page 8)
1/4 pound smoked Norwegian
  salmon, julienne-sliced in
  1/4-inch strips
Basil

Prepare 1 batch of Egg Pasta, adding the Classic Basil Pesto with the eggs and oil. Knead as usual, by hand or machine. Roll and cut about 1/4-inch wide to make tagliatelle noodles. Cook the noodles fresh, or gather bunches of the noodles into loose nests and dry on a dish towel or cake rack. When dry, the pasta bundles can be stored under refrigeration or frozen in plastic bags.

In a saucepan, melt 2 tablespoons of the butter. Sauté the shallots over low heat for 2 to 3 minutes. Add the cream and freshly ground pepper and continue to simmer until the cream is reduced to about half.

Meanwhile, bring 4 quarts of water to a boil in a large pot. Salt the water. Stir in the noodles and bring to a boil again. Fresh pasta cooks in 2 to 3 minutes, so check for doneness frequently.

When the cream is reduced, stir in the

pesto and the sliced smoked salmon.

Drain the pasta when done. Return to the warm pan and toss with the remaining 1 tablespoon of butter. Divide the pasta among 6 warm plates and spoon the salmon cream sauce over the noodles. Garnish with fresh opal or green basil sprigs.

Yield: 6 servings

Chinese Noodles with Cilantro Dressing

4 quarts water
1 pound fresh Chinese wheat and
    egg noodles
1-1/2 tablespoons sesame oil
3/4 cup Cilantro Pesto (page 15)
1/4 cup peanut oil
1/4 cup rice wine vinegar
2 tablespoons lemon juice
1/2 cup thinly sliced scallions,
    including some green
2 teaspoons black sesame seeds
Salt
4 teaspoons rice vinegar or to taste
l/8 to 1/4 teaspoon hot chili oil (or
    more to your taste)
Italian flat parsley or cilantro leaves

These noodles make a delightful side dish with grilled meats in the summer. Or serve them as a light first course with a Chinese meal.

Many supermarkets across the country carry Chinese wheat and egg noodles in their produce sections. Look for black sesame seeds with macrobiotic foods or with Japanese foods. This dish is not the same without them.

Bring the water to a boil in a large pot. Add the noodles and cook until just tender, about 8 minutes. Drain and rinse in cold water. Drain well and toss with the sesame oil. Set aside.

Whisk together the pesto, peanut oil, rice wine vinegar, and the lemon juice. Add the dressing, scallions, and black sesame seeds to the noodles and toss well. Season to taste with salt. Refrigerate for a few hours or overnight.

Just before serving, stir in the remaining 4 teaspoons rice vinegar and a few drops of hot chili oil to taste. Garnish with Italian flat parsley or fresh cilantro leaves.

Yield: 4 to 6 servings

Vermicelli with Red Pesto

3 quarts water
1/2 pound fresh vermicelli
1 tablespoon salt
2 tablespoons heavy cream
About 1 tablespoon hot pasta water
1/2 cup Red Basil Pesto (page 8)
1/2 cup minced smoked turkey
Freshly grated Parmesan cheese
Very finely slivered sun-dried
   tomatoes (page 26)

Bring the water to a boil in a deep saucepan. Add pasta and salt. Stir with a wooden fork or spoon to separate the strands. Boil rapidly, until just barely tender. To test, lift out a piece and taste.

Stir the cream and 1 tablespoon of the hot pasta water into the pesto. Drain the pasta and return it to the hot pan. Toss with the pesto and smoked turkey. Serve garnished with freshly grated Parmesan cheese and slivered sun-dried tomatoes.

Yield: 4 first course servings

3.
For Openers: Appetizers, Soups, Salads, and Breads

Stuffed Cherry Tomatoes

**30 to 40 ripe cherry tomatoes
(about 1-1/2 pints)**
**4 ounces cream cheese, at room
temperature**
**3 tablespoons Red Basil Pesto
(page 8)**
1 tablespoon minced scallions
About 1 teaspoon lemon juice
Salt and cayenne
Opal basil

Wash the tomatoes and cut a thin slice from the stem end of each. Scoop out the seeds and set aside to drain upside down.

Combine the cream cheese, pesto, scallions, and lemon juice. Season to taste with salt and cayenne. Fill the tomato shells with the pesto mixture and refrigerate. Serve garnished with sprigs of opal basil leaves.

Yield: 8 to 10 servings

Red Basil Torta

**About 2 pounds Mascarpone cheese
(or Italian triple crème cheese)**
1/2 cup Red Basil Pesto (page 8)
2 to 3 tablespoons pine nuts

Mascarpone is a fresh Italian cheese, rich and buttery. Layered with Red Pesto and pine nuts it makes a delectable first course.

Horizontally slice the Mascarpone cheese into slices 1/2 to 5/8 inch thick. Spread a slice of the cheese with the pesto and sprinkle with pine nuts. Spread another slice with the pesto and nuts and stack over the first layer. Continue spreading and layering. Finish with a top layer of Mascarpone with pine nuts sprinkled thickly on the top. Cover with plastic wrap and chill.

After chilling, trim the sides with a sharp knife or a wire cheese cutter and rewrap. Serve at room temperature with crackers.

The torta may be frozen. Defrost the wrapped torta at room temperature before serving.

Yield: 8 to 10 first course servings

Pesto Stuffed Mushrooms

18 large mushrooms
2 tablespoons butter
1/3 cup minced scallions, including
    some green tops
2 tablespoons Garlic Thyme Pesto
    (page 29)
2 tablespoons port wine
1/2 cup fresh bread crumbs
1/4 cup minced fresh parsley
1/4 cup grated Jarlsburg cheese (or
    any good Swiss-type cheese)
2 tablespoons freshly grated
    Parmesan cheese
Approximately 2 tablespoons heavy
    cream
Salt and freshly ground pepper
3 tablespoons melted butter
1 tablespoon grated Jarlsburg

The pesto and port wine give these mushrooms a delicious flavor. The recipe should make 6 servings but, then again, it might serve 2.

Wipe the mushrooms with a damp cloth and trim the stem. Carefully break the stems from the cap and finely chop the stems.

Melt 2 tablespoons butter in a sauté pan, and sauté the scallions and chopped mushroom stems for 3 to 4 minutes, until slightly soft.

Add the pesto and the port. Simmer for approximately 2 minutes, until the port has reduced by half. Remove from the pan and let cool for 5 minutes.

Add the fresh bread crumbs, parsley, and the cheeses to the pesto mixture. Add just enough cream to lightly bind the mixture together. Season to taste with salt and pepper.

Dip the outside of the caps in the 3 tablespoons melted butter and mound the stuffing lightly in the center. Top with the remaining 1 tablespoon grated Jarlsburg cheese and drizzle the caps with the remaining melted butter. Place close together in a shallow baking dish and bake uncovered at 375° for 15-20 minutes. Serve warm.

Yield: 2 to 6 servings

Red Pesto Ceviche

1 pound bay, cape, or sea scallops
(sea scallops should be sliced in
thirds across the grain)
1 teaspoon salt
3/4 cup fresh lime juice
1/3 cup minced scallions
1/4 cup Red Basil Pesto (page 8)
1/2 teaspoon crushed chili peppers
1 teaspoon dried oregano or
1 tablespoon minced fresh
oregano
1 large bay leaf, crumbled
1/4 cup olive oil
1/4 cup sliced stuffed olives
1 cup diced seeded ripe tomatoes
1/4 cup minced Italian flat parsley

Ceviche calls for the freshest of seafood. The fish retains a tender, fresh quality because the lime juice does the "cooking." Serve as a first course or hors d'oeuvre.

Place the scallops in a nonaluminum bowl. Add the salt, lime juice, and scallions. Stir to combine gently and refrigerate for at least 3 to 4 hours, preferably overnight.

Drain, reserving 1/2 cup of the marinade. Combine the 1/2 cup marinade with the pesto, chili peppers, oregano, bay leaf, and olive oil. Add to the scallops along with the olives, tomatoes, and parsley. Taste and adjust the seasoning. Serve cold.

Yield: 4 to 6 servings

Seafood with Creamy Tarragon Sauce

1/4 cup Creamy Tarragon Pesto (page 25)
6 tablespoons Crème Fraîche (page 124)
Lemon juice
Salt
Bibb lettuce leaves
1/2 pound smoked trout or smoked eel
Lemon wedges
Nasturtiums

Combine the pesto, Crème Fraîche, a little lemon juice, and salt to taste. Arrange the lettuce and seafood on individual serving plates. Spoon a few tablespoons of the sauce over the seafood. Garnish with lemon wedges and nasturtiums.

Yield: 4 servings

Crab Meat with Rosy Crème Fraîche

6 ounces fresh crab meat
1 tablespoon fresh lemon or lime
   juice
Salt
1/4 cup Crème Fraîche (page 124)
2 tablespoons Red Basil Pesto (page
   8)
Lemon or lime juice
Salt and freshly ground pepper
Red leaf lettuce, cherry tomatoes,
   red salmon caviar, or crackers

Pick over the crab meat for any remaining cartilage. Toss gently with 1 tablespoon lemon or lime juice and a little salt. Set aside.

To make the Rosy Crème Fraîche, stir the crème fraîche into the pesto. Taste for seasoning and add just a little lemon or lime juice, salt, and pepper.

Serve the crab meat on red leaf lettuce topped with the Rosy Crème Fraîche. Or fill hollowed-out cherry tomatoes with the crab meat and top with the sauce. Or mound the crab meat in a small bowl. Top with Rosy Crème Fraîche and garnish with red salmon caviar. Surround with crackers for a cocktail hor d'oeuvre.

Yield: 4 appetizer servings or 8 to 10 cocktail servings

VARIATION
   Poach sea scallops in salted water to cover for 1 minute. Remove from heat and let cool in poaching liquid. Drain and serve with Rosy Crème Fraîche as you would the crab meat.

Shrimp with Cold Cilantro Sauce

1-1/2 cups water
1 bay leaf, crumbled
3 or 4 lemon slices, halved
1/4 teaspoon salt
8 jumbo raw shrimp
2 tablespoons Cilantro Pesto (page 15)
2 tablespoons sour cream
2 tablespoons mayonnaise
1 teaspoon lime juice
Salt
Small Bibb lettuce leaves
1 ripe avocado, sliced
Lime slices
Cilantro leaves

Bring the water, bay leaf, lemon slices, and salt to a boil. Rinse the shrimp and add to the seasoned boiling water. Simmer, covered, for 3 to 5 minutes, until the shrimp are just cooked through. Remove the shrimp with a slotted spoon. Shell and devein, cover, and refrigerate.

Combine the pesto, sour cream, mayonnaise, and lime juice in a small bowl. Add salt to taste.

Arrange the shrimp and avocado slices on the lettuce. Spoon the cilantro sauce over the shrimp. Garnish with lime slices and cilantro leaves.

Yield: 2 servings

VARIATIONS
Cooked crab claws or poached scallops can be substituted for the shrimp.

Mussel Soup with Mediterranean Pesto

3 pounds mussels in their shells
2 large garlic cloves, minced
1 small onion, chopped
1 bay leaf, crumbled
3/4 cup dry white wine or dry
    vermouth
1 cup water
1/4 cup olive oil
6 to 8 large shallots, chopped (or
    substitute 2 medium-size onions)
3 medium-size ripe tomatoes,
    chopped (or 1-1/2 cups canned
    Italian plum tomatoes, drained)
1/2 cup tomato puree
2 tablespoons Mediterranean Pesto
    (page 18) or any basil pesto, or
    Garlic Thyme Pesto (page 29),
    Savory Pesto (page 22), or
    Fennel Pesto (page 16)
Salt and freshly ground pepper
Chopped fresh parsley

This makes a hearty meal served with French bread rubbed with a cut garlic clove and sautéed in olive oil. Add a salad to complete the meal.

Scrub the mussels well and remove the stringy beard with a knife. A soapless scouring pad works well for scrubbing. Discard any mussels that remain open. Mussels must be *very* fresh and used within 1 day of purchase.

In a large saucepan, combine the mussels, garlic, onion, bay leaf, wine and water. Shake to distribute the mussels and steam for about 3 to 4 minutes, just until the mussels open. Remove the opened mussels, discarding any that are closed. Strain the broth through 2 thicknesses of dampened cheese cloth and set aside.

Heat the olive oil in a large heavy skillet, and sauté the shallots until softened. Add the strained mussel broth slowly, leaving any remaining sediment in the pan. Cook rapidly for 4 or 5 minutes to reduce the volume and intensify the flavor. Add the remaining ingredients and simmer for about 5 minutes. Remove the mussels from the shells and add to the soup and taste for seasoning. Sprinkle a little chopped parsley to garnish each soup bowl.

Yield: 4 servings

VARIATION

A cup of small bay scallops or any seafood are a nice addition. A cup of dry red wine can be added to taste.

Chilled Cucumber Pesto Soup

2 cups peeled, seeded, and diced
   cucumber
1/2 cup Creamy Basil Pesto (page
   13)
1-1/2 cups plain yogurt
1/2 cup sour cream
2 tablespoons rice or white vinegar
About 1/4 teaspoon salt
White pepper
Basil or parsley

You may wish to add 1 small garlic clove to the soup for extra flavor. The long, seedless cucumbers make the preparation a breeze.

Combine the cucumber, pesto, yogurt, sour cream, vinegar, and salt in a food processor or blender. Blend until smooth. Taste, add white pepper, and adjust the seasoning. Serve very cold, garnished with basil or parsley.

Yield: 4 servings

Sorrel Soup

2 tablespoons butter
1/2 cup diced onion
1-3/4 cups grated unpeeled zucchini
1/2 cup Sorrel Basil Pesto (page 11)
1-1/2 cups chicken broth
Salt and freshly ground pepper

This soup makes an elegant hot first course or a cold light lunch. Try making it with wild sorrel, too.

Melt the butter in a large saucepan and sauté the onion and zucchini for 4 to 5 minutes, until just tender. Do not brown. Add the pesto and 1/2 cup of the chicken broth. Bring to a simmer and remove from the heat.

Purée the soup in a food processor or blender. Return to the saucepan and add the remaining 1 cup chicken broth. Season to taste with salt and freshly ground pepper. Serve warm or cold.

Yield: 4 servings

Fruit Salad with Cilantro Dressing

About 2 cups garden lettuce (romaine, curly, or leaf lettuce)
1/3 cup walnuts
2 cups water
1 cup celery, thinly sliced on the diagonal
2 tablespoons Cilantro Pesto (page 151)
1 tablespoon lemon juice
3 tablespoons walnut oil
Salt
2 large oranges, peeled and sliced 1/4 inch thick
2 medium-size ripe avocados, peeled and sliced
2 kiwi fruit, peeled and sliced 1/4inch thick

Wash and dry the lettuce leaves.

Toast the walnuts in a 300°F. oven for about 10 minutes, until light brown.

Bring the water to a boil and add the celery. Simmer over a high heat for 2 minutes. Drain and refresh the celery with cold water.

Whisk together the pesto, lemon juice, and walnut oil. Add salt to taste.

Arrange the lettuce leaves on individual serving plates. Top with the sliced fruit, celery, and toasted walnuts. Pour the cilantro dressing over the salad and serve cold.

Yield: 4 servings

Red Coleslaw with Mint Dressing

3 tablespoons Winter Mint Pesto
   (page 35)
2 tablespoons rice or white vinegar
2 tablespoons safflower oil
1/2 teaspoon sugar
1/4 teaspoon salt
2 cups grated carrots (2 to 3
   carrots)
2 cups grated red cabbage
2 to 3 tablespoons minced scallions,
   including some green
Red leaf lettuce
2 large oranges, peeled, sliced
   horizontally, and quartered

This rosy coleslaw with the zing of mint pesto in the dressing makes a great winter salad.

Whisk together the pesto, vinegar, oil, sugar, and salt.

Combine the carrots, cabbage, and scallions with the dressing and taste for seasoning. Chill.

Arrange the lettuce on individual salad plates. Top with the coleslaw and garnish with orange slices. Serve cold.

Yield: 4 to 6 servings

Warm Goat Cheese Salad

6 to 8 ounces fresh goat cheese
3 tablespoons Classic Basil Pesto
   (page 7) or Mediterranean Pesto
   (page 18)
1 cup fine dry bread crumbs
1/4 cup roughly chopped or broken
   walnuts
1 tablespoon high-quality whole
   grain mustard
3 tablespoons herb vinegar (a local-
   ly produced tarragon or mixed
   herb vinegar would be my choice)
6 tablespoons walnut oil
Salt and freshly cracked pepper
1/2 small sweet red pepper, julienne
   sliced
Mixed young greens (oak leaf and
   red leaf lettuces, Belgian endive,
   watercress, or spinach)

This is a pesto variation of a classic California salad. The goat cheese is spread with pesto, dipped in bread crumbs, then heated briefly. The delicious, warm, soft cheese center contrasts nicely with the cool greens and the tangy, walnut vinaigrette. It is worth searching for a good fresh local goat cheese, as well as a local herb vinegar and mustard.

Preheat the oven to 300°F.

Slice the goat cheese into 6 slices about 1/2-inch thick and about 1-3/4 inches square or round. Spread both sides of the cheese with a thin layer of pesto. Dip in dry bread crumbs to coat on all sides and place on a lightly oiled baking dish.

Toast the walnuts in the 300°F. oven for about 10 minutes to bring out the natural oils.

Whisk together the mustard, vinegar, and the walnut oil. Season well with salt and freshly cracked pepper. Add the hot toasted walnuts. Taste and adjust for seasoning.

Reset the oven to 400°F. Bake the cheese for 8 to 10 minutes, until soft and lightly brown.

Arrange the greens and red pepper on salad plates and place a slice of warm goat cheese in the center of each. Spoon the walnut vinaigrette over all. Serve at once.

Yield: 6 servings

Fresh Tuna Green Bean Salad

1 pound fresh tuna fillet, 1 inch
   thick
2 tablespoons minced red onion
6 tablespoons Mediterranean Pesto
   (page 18 or page 31)
6 tablespoons lemon juice
6 tablespoons olive oil
2 cups water
1 cup sliced fresh green beans, cut
   in 1/2-inch pieces
1 tablespoon finely julienned sun-
   dried tomatoes
Freshly ground pepper
1 pound freshly cooked pasta
Plum tomatoes

The sweet mild tastes of fresh tuna and green beans are enhanced by the herbs in the pungent Mediterranean Pesto (rosemary, thyme, savory, and oregano). Pasta shells or a corkscrew fusilli will soak up and hold the delicious flavors of the pesto.

Slice the fresh tuna horizontally to 1/2 inch thickness. Then slice in thin slices, about 1/4 inch wide. Place in a nonmetallic dish with the red onion.

Whisk together the pesto, lemon juice, and olive oil. Pour over the tuna and onion. Marinate for 20 to 30 minutes.

Heat a large sauté pan, and with a slotted spoon, place the tuna in a single layer in the hot pan. Sauté briefly, reducing the heat after a minute or two. The tuna cooks very quickly. Sauté only until the fish flakes, about 2 or 3 minutes. Remove from the heat to a warm serving dish. Cover with any remaining marinade.

Bring the water to a boil and blanch the beans for 3 or 4 minutes, until just done and still crunchy. Drain.

Combine the tuna, beans, and sun-dried tomatoes. Add pepper to taste. Gently combine with the pasta, chill, and serve cold. Garnish with sliced ripe plum tomatoes.

Yield: 4 servings

Pesto Pasta Salad

1 pound fusilli (spiral) or small
    shell pasta
1 cup green beans, cut diagonally
    1/4-inch long, or broccoli florets
    and sliced stems
2/3 cup julienne-sliced carrots
1/3 cup minced red onion or sliced
    scallions
1-1/2 cups cherry tomatoes,
    quartered
1 cup any basil pesto (pages 7 to
    14) or Anchovy Herb Pesto (page
    36) or Mediterranean Pesto (page
    18)
1/4 cup safflower oil
2 tablespoons fresh lemon juice
1/4 cup wine vinegar
Salt and freshly ground pepper

This recipe was developed for a friend's wedding. She multiplied the recipe by 15, using a whole crate of basil to make 15 cups of pesto. The results were about 12 gallons of salad, more than enough to feed 150 people on a sunny June day.

In a large pot of boiling salted water, cook the pasta for 10 to 12 minutes, or until just tender. Drain. Immerse in cold water to stop the cooking process and drain again.

Steam the green beans or broccoli and carrots for about 2 minutes until tender-crisp. Immerse in cold water to stop the cooking and drain.

Whisk together the pesto, oil, lemon juice, and vinegar.

In a large bowl combine the vegetables, pasta, and dressing. Add salt and freshly

ground pepper liberally to taste. The salad
may be served cold or at room temperature.

Yield: 8 to 10 servings

VARIATIONS
   Add or substitute peas, chopped zucchini, summer
squash or cucumbers. Crumbled feta cheese or chopped parsley are also good additions.

Salad of Barley and Snow Peas

4 cups water
1-1/4 cups uncooked pearl barley
1/2 cup broken walnuts
1/2 cup Anchovy Herb Pesto (page 36)
1 tablespoon whole-grain mustard
2 tablespoons tarragon vinegar
1/3 cup fresh lemon juice
2 tablespoons olive oil
Salt and freshly ground pepper
1/4 cup sliced scallions, including some green tops
1 cup diced celery
2 cups diced ripe tomatoes
2 cups snow peas or sugar snap peas (approximately 1/2 pound)

Take this salad on a picnic with some good bread and whatever crudités are in season. As a variation, you might add some crumbled Montrachet or feta cheese, or a few shrimp.

Bring the water to a boil and add the barley. Cover and simmer for about 30 minutes, until the barley is just tender. Drain and rinse with cold water. Drain well.

Toast the walnuts on a cookie sheet in a 300°F. oven for 12 to 15 minutes, until the oils are released and the nuts achieve a good toasted flavor.

Whisk together the pesto, mustard, vinegar, lemon juice, olive oil, salt, and pepper.

Combine the barley, scallions, celery, walnuts, and anchovy pesto dressing. Fold in the diced tomatoes and taste for seasoning. Chill.

String the peas and slice in 1/2-inch dices. Steam over boiling water for about 3 minutes. Refresh in cold water to stop the cooking process. Drain and refrigerate.

Fold the pea pods into the salad just before serving. This dish can be eaten cold or at room temperature.

Yield: 6 to 8 servings

Spring Potato Asparagus Salad

3 cups water
6 cups new red potatoes, sliced
   1/4-inch thick
1/2 cup Anchovy Herb Pesto (page
   36)
2 tablespoons whole-grain mustard
1 tablespoon tarragon vinegar
3 tablespoons fresh lemon juice
6 tablespoons olive oil
2 tablespoons freshly grated
   Parmesan cheese
8 to 10 ounces smoked trout (1
   small trout)
1 to 1-1/2 pounds asparagus, cut in
   3/4-inch pieces (2 to 3 cups)
Salt and freshly ground black
   pepper

Excellent smoked fish is readily available in this country now, and the popular new smokers have made it easy for people to smoke their own catch. The red-skinned new potatoes, fresh green asparagus, and trout, combined with the green of the pesto dressing make a colorful springtime combination.

Bring the water to a boil. Add the potatoes and cook until barely tender, but firm to the bite, 5 to 7 minutes. Drain the potatoes very well.

Whisk together the pesto, mustard, vinegar, lemon juice, olive oil, and cheese. Fold about two-thirds of the dressing into the potatoes, keeping the potatoes as whole as possible. Cover and set aside.

Carefully remove the skin and small bones from the trout and break the meat into bite-size pieces approximately 3/4-inch square. Fold into the potatoes. Chill.

Steam the asparagus over boiling water until barely tender, 3 to 5 minutes. It should be bright green and crunchy. Refresh in cold water. Drain well and chill.

Fold the asparagus into the potatoes about 30 minutes before you wish to serve the salad. Spoon the salad onto a serving platter or bowl. I like to serve this salad on a fish platter, garnished with red and green leaf lettuce and sunflower seed sprouts. Pour the remaining pesto dressing over the top.

Yield: 6 to 8 servings

French Country Salad

3 tablespoons Tarragon Pesto (page 24)
1 tablespoon whole-grain mustard
3 tablespoons tarragon vinegar
6 tablespoons olive oil
Salt and freshly ground pepper
1 tablespoon olive oil
1 chicken breast, split
Water
1-1/2 to 2 cups quartered, sliced new potatoes
1-1/2 to 2 cups fresh green beans, cut in 1-inch pieces
Bibb lettuce

Whisk together the pesto, mustard, vinegar, and 6 tablespoons olive oil. Season to taste with salt and freshly ground pepper. Set aside. Heat the remaining 1 tablespoon olive oil in a small pan. Add the chicken and sauté on both sides.

Add a few tablespoons of water, partially cover, and simmer until tender. Tear the meat into bite-size pieces (about 1/2 inch by 2 inches).

Steam the new potatoes and green beans in a vegetable steamer over boiling water until just tender, about 10 minutes.

Fold the dressing into the chicken and vegetables. Marinate for at least 30 minutes. Spoon the salad onto a bed of lettuce. Serve cold or at room temperature.

Yield: 4 servings

VARIATIONS
   Add sliced raw mushrooms or toasted walnuts for crunch. Add sliced ripe tomatoes and a cold white zinfandel for a picnic.

Pasta Seafood Salad

4 quarts water
Salt
1 pound fusilli or small shell pasta
Olive oil
1 pound cape or bay scallops
2-1/2 cups court bouillon or 2-1/2
   cups clam juice
6 ounces fresh crab meat (optional)
1 tablespoon minced red onion
2 cups diced peeled ripe tomatoes,
   well-drained
1/2 cup chopped fresh parsley
   leaves
2 cups Anchovy Herb Dressing
   (page 98)
Red leaf lettuce
Lemon wedges

Combine the water and salt in a large pot and bring to a boil. Cook the pasta until it is *al dente*. Drain thoroughly, and toss with a small amount of olive oil. Set aside.

Rinse the scallops. Bring the court bouillon or clam juice to a simmer. Add the scallops and poach for 3-4 minutes, until just cooked (no more). Drain the scallops and cool briefly on a large cold plate. Add to the pasta.

Pick through the crab meat for any cartilage. Add the crab meat, red onion, tomatoes, and parsley to the pasta and scallops. Combine with the Anchovy Herb Dressing and toss gently.

Serve on a bed of red leaf lettuce and garnish with lemon wedges.

Yield: 8 servings

Tomatoes Stuffed with Pesto Pasta

1 teaspoon salt
Boiling water
1/2 pound vermicelli
3 tablespoons Anchovy Herb Pesto
   (page 36)
1 tablespoon lemon juice
1 tablespoon tarragon vinegar
2 tablespoons olive oil
2 tablespoons pine nuts
Salt and freshly ground pepper
6 to 8 medium-size ripe tomatoes
Lettuce leaves
About 2 tablespoons crumbled
   Montrachet or feta cheese

Add the salt to a large pot of boiling water. Add the vermicelli and cook over high heat for 8 to 10 minutes, until just cooked *al dente*. Drain well. Rinse with cold water and drain thoroughly. With a pair of kitchen scissors, cut the vermicelli into short lengths, about 2 inches long.

Whisk together the pesto, lemon juice, vinegar, and olive oil. In a large bowl, combine the vermicelli and dressing. Add the pine nuts and season to taste with salt and pepper.

Remove a thin slice from the stem end of each tomato. Hollow out the centers of the tomatoes and drain upside down. Stuff the tomato shells with the pasta and chill. Serve on lettuce leaves garnished with the crumbled cheese.

Yield: 6 to 8 servings

Tabbouleh with Mint Pesto

1-1/2 cups dry bulgur
3 cups boiling water
1 teaspoon salt
2 or more tablespoons Mint Pesto
  (page 10 or 35)
2 tablespoons tarragon vinegar
1-1/2 tablespoons fresh lemon juice
2 tablespoons olive oil
2 teaspoons whole-grain mustard
1/4 cup chopped parsley leaves
1/4 cup chopped scallions,
  including some green
3 tablespoons crumbled feta cheese
1 cup diced peeled cucumber
1 cup diced ripe tomato
Mint leaves
Romaine lettuce

With Mint Pesto you can have tabbouleh in any season. Freeze the Mint Pesto in small batches so you can pull out just what you need.

Combine the bulgur, boiling water, and salt in a large bowl. Cover and let stand for 20 to 30 minutes, until the bulgur has softened.

Meanwhile, whisk together the pesto, vinegar, lemon juice, olive oil, mustard, and parsley.

Drain the bulgur well. Add the dressing, scallions, feta cheese, cucumber, and tomato. Mix thoroughly and refrigerate for 1 hour or more. Retaste and adjust the seasoning. Add minced fresh mint if you wish. Serve on a bed of romaine garnished with mint leaves.

Yield: 4 to 6 servings

Braided Pesto Herb Bread

2 tablespoons dry baker's yeast
1 tablespoon sugar
1/2 cup warm water
3 cups unbleached all-purpose flour
1/2 teaspoon salt
1 tablespoon crumbled dry sage
1/2 cup whole milk ricotta
6 tablespoons Mediterranean Pesto
  (page 18)
1 tablespoon high-quality whole
  grain mustard
2 large eggs
1/2 cup chopped fresh parsley
  leaves
1/4 cup pine nuts
1 small egg
1/2 teaspoon salt
2 tablespoons chopped pine nuts

This recipe has become a favorite of mine. The pesto, ricotta, mustard, and pine nuts give this unusual bread a distinctive aroma and tender, moist quality; and it is easily mixed in a food processor. The false braid makes a big, handsome loaf. Serve it with a hearty soup and salad to make a distinctive meal.

In a small bowl, dissolve the yeast and the sugar in the warm water. Let stand until foamy and dissolved, about 5 minutes.

Insert the metal blade in the food processor and add the flour, salt, sage, ricotta, pesto, and mustard. Process for about 20 seconds.

Whisk the 2 large eggs and combine with the yeast mixture. With the motor running, pour the yeast mixture through the feed tube, and process until the dough is smooth and cleans the sides of the bowl. If the dough is too moist to clean the sides of the bowl, add flour by the tablespoon through the feed tube until the dough forms a ball. Process for about 30 seconds to knead the dough. Add the parsley and ¼ cup pine nuts through the feed tube and process just to mix.

Place the dough in a lightly oiled bowl, turning to coat all sides. Cover with oiled plastic wrap and a towel. Set to rise in a warm place until the dough has doubled in bulk, 45 to 60 minutes.

Punch down the dough and knead briefly on a lightly floured board. I like to make this bread into what is called a "false plait," but it can be baked in two 4-inch by 8-1/4-inch loaf pans. For the plaited loaf, roll the dough out on a lightly floured board to a rectangle measuring about 9 inches by 13 inches. Cut 3-1/2-inch slices on a diagonal all the way up both 13 inch sides, leaving a solid 2-inch center of dough. The slices should be about 3/4-inch wide. Starting at one end, fold the slices up over the middle section of dough, overlapping pieces and alternating sides. Tuck the ends in. Place on an oiled baking sheet.

Make an egg wash by beating 1 small egg with ½ teaspoon salt. Brush the loaf with the egg wash and sprinkle the remaining 2 tablespoons chopped pine nuts over the top.

Cover loosely with oiled plastic wrap and set in a warm place to rise until almost doubled, 30 to 40 minutes. Meanwhile, preheat the oven to 375°F.

Bake for 30 to 35 minutes until the loaf sounds hollow when tapped. Remove to a rack. Serve warm.

Yield: 1 large braided loaf or 2 medium-size loaves

Anchovy Herb Dressing

1/4 cup Anchovy Herb Pesto (page 36)
2 tablespoons fresh lemon juice
2 teaspoons tarragon vinegar
2 tablespoons olive oil
2 tablespoons safflower oil
2 teaspoons freshly grated Parmesan cheese (optional)
Freshly ground pepper
Small amount of salt

Surround a small bowl of this pungent sauce with crudités as an appetizer. Or dress lightly steamed summer squash, zucchini, and tomato with this dressing and butter. It also makes a good salad dressing for greens, new potatoes, and pasta.

Whisk together the pesto, lemon juice, vinegar, olive oil, safflower oil, and cheese. Season carefully with salt and freshly ground pepper.

Yield: About 2/3 cup

4.
Entrees

Summer Vegetable Gratin

2 cups diced summer squash
(1/2-inch dices)
2 cups diced zucchini (1/2-inch
dices)
2 tablespoons minced red onion or
scallion
1 cup diced ripe tomatoes
2 tablespoons butter
2 tablespoons Cilantro Pesto (page
15) or Oregano Thyme Pesto
(page 28)
Salt and freshly ground pepper
1/2 cup grated cheddar or
Monterey jack cheese

Steam the summer squash and zucchini until barely tender, 5 to 6 minutes. Combine with the onion and tomatoes in a large bowl. Preheat the oven to 350°F.

Melt the butter and add to the pesto. Pour over the vegetables. Add salt and pepper to taste and toss lightly. Transfer to a low-sided gratin dish. Cover with foil and bake for 20 minutes. Remove from the oven and top with grated cheese. Bake uncovered until lightly brown, about 5 minutes. Serve hot.

Yield: 4 servings

VARIATION
Add 1 cup fresh-cut corn from the cob to the squash and tomatoes.

Corn-on-the-Cob with Cilantro Butter

1/4 cup Cilantro Pesto (page 15)
1/4 cup butter at room temperature
Lime juice
Salt and freshly ground pepper
3 quarts water
1/2 teaspoon sugar
8 ears fresh corn

Cilantro butter has an unusual smoky flavor that is delicious with corn-on-the-cob.

Combine the pesto with the soft butter in a small bowl. Add lime juice, salt, and freshly ground pepper to taste.

Bring 3 quarts of unsalted water to a boil in a large, covered pot. Shuck the corn of silk and husks. Add the sugar and corn to the boiling water. Boil 6 to 8 minutes, depending on size and freshness of the corn. Or soak the ears in water, remove the silk and grill over charcoal, turning frequently. Serve immediately with the cilantro butter.

Yield: 4 servings

Pesto Soubise

2 quarts salted water
1/3 cup uncooked long-grain white
　　rice
2 tablespoons butter
1/2 cup Savory Pesto (page 22) or
　　Classic Basil Pesto (page 7)
4 cups roughly chopped yellow
　　onions (2 to 3 large onions)
Freshly ground pepper and a little
　　salt
1/4 cup grated Swiss cheese
1/4 cup light cream

Bring the water to a rolling boil. Add the rice and boil uncovered for exactly 5 minutes. Drain and set aside.

Preheat the oven to 325°F.

Melt the butter with the pesto in a very large pan. Stir in the chopped onions, rice, and freshly ground pepper and salt. Mix well, until all is coated with the butter-pesto mixture.

Turn into a shallow 1-1/2 quart baking dish. Cover tightly with heavy foil and bake for 40 to 50 minutes, stirring once or twice, until the rice is tender.

Remove and stir in grated cheese and cream. Taste and season with salt and pepper. Serve warm.

Yield: 4 to 6 servings

Mussels with Green Sorrel Sauce

4 pounds very fresh large mussels
3/4 cup Sorrel Pesto With Lemon
(page 23)

The key to flavor is freshness. Buy and cook mussels the day they arrive at your fish market. Allow 3/4 pound of mussels per person. The sauce can be kept frozen.

Scrub the mussels well under cool running water and pull loose the fibrous beard. Discard any open mussels. Bring about 2 inches of water to a boil in a large covered pan. Add the mussels and simmer for 3 to 4 minutes until they open. Taste for doneness. Larger mussels will take longer to cook than the small ones. Drain in a colander, discarding any mussels that have not opened.

Pull the shells apart; discard the top shell. Arrange the opened shells on serving plates. Spoon 1/2 to 3/4 teaspoon of the pesto over each mussel. Serve hot or cold.

Yield: 4 to 6 servings

Bay Scallops with Lemon Thyme Crumbs

1-1/3 pounds fresh bay scallops
1 small lemon
1/4 cup sweet butter, at room
    temperature
1/4 cup Lemon Thyme Pesto (page
    32)
1/2 to 2/3 cup dry bread crumbs
Salt
Lemon wedges

This dish works equally well as a first course or as a main course with a risotto and fresh broccoli. Accompany with a chilled, light Soave and fresh fruit for a satisfying light supper.

Preheat the oven to 450°F.

Place the scallops in a single layer in a lightly oiled baking dish. Squeeze lemon juice over all.

Whisk together the butter and pesto in a small bowl. Add enough bread crumbs to achieve a crumbly texture. Season to taste with salt. Spoon the topping over the scallops.

Bake until just hot and bubbly, approximately 10 minutes.

Serve hot with lemon wedges on the side.

Yield: 4 main course servings or 6 to 8 first course servings

Grilled Swordfish with Cilantro Sauce

1/4 cup Cilantro Pesto (page 15)
1/4 cup lime juice
1/4 cup olive oil
2 cups diced peeled ripe tomatoes
Salt and freshly ground pepper
4 swordfish steaks, 3/4-inch thick
   (about 1/3 pound each

Swordfish lends itself to barbecuing. The marinade gives it a tart, delicate, smoky flavor.

Combine the pesto, lime juice, olive oil, tomatoes, salt, and freshly ground pepper in a small bowl.

Place the swordfish pieces in a shallow glass or nonaluminum dish and cover with the marinade. Marinate for 2 hours or more in the refrigerator, turning the fish at least once.

Prepare the fire in the grill. Brush the grill with oil and prepare it for medium-heat grilling. Grill the swordfish about 5 minutes on each side until the fish tests done.

Heat the remaining marinade in a saucepan. Pour over the swordfish steaks and serve hot.

Yield: 4 servings

Baked Sole with Pesto Sauce

2 tablespoons butter
1 tablespoon olive oil
1/2 cup minced scallions
1 large shallot, minced
1-1/2 cups chopped mushrooms
Salt and pepper
1 pound sole fillets
1/2 cup Winter Lemon Thyme
   Pesto (page 32), Fennel Pesto
   (page 16), or other pesto
About 3 tablespoons light cream

Preheat the oven to 350°F.

In a sauté pan, heat the butter and oil and sauté the scallions and shallot for 2 minutes. Add the chopped mushrooms and continue to sauté until the mushrooms begin to soften. Season to taste with salt and pepper.

Layer half the sole fillets in a lightly oiled, low-sided baking dish. Cover with the scallions and mushrooms. Layer the remaining sole fillets on top and cover with foil. Bake for 15 minutes.

Meanwhile, combine the pesto with enough cream to make a thick pourable sauce. Cover the sole with the pesto sauce, return to the oven, and bake uncovered until the sauce is bubbly, about 5 minutes. Serve hot.

Yield: 4 servings

Grilled Monkfish

2 tablespoons Lemon Thyme Pesto
(page 32)
1 tablespoon lemon juice
2 tablespoons vegetable oil
2 tablespoons chopped scallions,
including some green
Salt and freshly ground black
pepper
1-1/2 pounds monkfish fillets, cut
in 1-1/2 inch pieces
1 sweet red pepper, seeded and
sliced
1 green pepper, seeded and sliced

VARIATIONS
A firm-fleshed white fish, such as halibut, swordfish, scrod, or red snapper, can be substituted for the
monkfish.

Lemon Thyme Pesto gives the monkfish a piquant, subtle flavor. Throw wet wood chips on the fire for added smokiness if desired.

Whisk together the pesto, lemon juice, vegetable oil, and scallions. Season to taste with salt and pepper. Marinate the monkfish in the pesto mixture for 2 to 3 hours, turning occasionally.

Prepare a fire in a grill. Skewer monkfish pieces alternately with slices of red and green peppers.

Oil the grill lightly to avoid sticking. Place the skewers on the grill. Grill for 6 to 8 minutes, brushing with the marinade, and turning occasionally. Test a piece of fish. It should be moist and tender.

Serve hot with any remaining marinade poured over the monkfish.

Yield: 4 to 6 servings

Sliced Pesto Chicken Breasts

4 boned, skinless chicken half--
   breasts (6 to 8 ounces each)
2/3 cup ricotta cheese
About 1/3 cup Thyme Pesto (page
   27), or Savory Pesto (page 22),
   or any basil pesto (pages 7-14)
1 teaspoon minced shallot
Salt and freshly ground pepper
8 or more large spinach leaves
1 cup all-purpose flour
Salt and pepper
2 tablespoons butter
2 tablespoons olive oil
Sweet Red Pepper Sauce (page 50)
   (optional)

This dish can be prepared ahead, sliced later, and served warm or cold. Serve with the Sweet Red Pepper Sauce for a stunning presentation.

Pound each chicken breast between 2 sturdy plastic bags with a rubber mallet, rolling pin, or heavy frying pan until very thin and about double in size.

Combine the ricotta, pesto, and shallot. Season to taste with salt and pepper. Add more pesto to taste, if desired.

Dip the spinach leaves in boiling water for 5 seconds. Remove the stem and some of the center vein with scissors and drain on towels.

To assemble the chicken breasts, lay each breast smooth side down. Cover with 2 or more spinach leaves and about 2 table-spoons of the pesto/ricotta mixture in a smooth, thin layer. Roll the breast tightly, starting at one of the long sides. Place the breasts tightly together, seam side down, in a dish. Cover with plastic wrap and refrigerate.

About 20 minutes before serving, combine the flour and salt and pepper to taste. Dredge the chicken rolls in the flour. Rechill for 10 minutes.

Preheat the oven to 350°F.

Heat the butter and oil in a large sauté pan. Brown the chicken rolls quickly over high heat on each side, about 1 minute per side. Place the rolls close together in a shallow baking dish and bake uncovered for 10 minutes, just until tender. Remove and set aside for 5 minutes. Slice crosswise into 3/4-inch slices. Serve warm with the Sweet Red Pepper Sauce or chill and serve cold.

Yield: 4 servings

Lamb Grilled with Pesto Marinade

1 tablespoon Classic Basil Pesto
(page 7)
1 tablespoon Oregano Pesto (page
19)
1/2 teaspoon fresh or dried
rosemary
1/2 teaspoon crushed chili peppers
1 tablespoon minced onion
2 tablespoons lemon juice
2 tablespoons olive oil
1-1/4 to 1-1/2 pounds boneless
lamb (from the leg), cut in 1-inch
pieces
1 sweet red pepper, cut in 1-inch
pieces
1 green pepper, cut in 1-inch pieces

In a small bowl, whisk together the basil and oregano pestos, rosemary, crushed chili peppers, minced onion, lemon juice, and olive oil until blended. Add the lamb and stir to coat with marinade. Cover and refrigerate for 30 to 45 minutes, stirring occasionally. Bring to room temperature before grilling.

Prepare the fire in the grill. Thread the meat onto skewers alternating with red and green pepper pieces. Oil the grill.

Grill the lamb 4 to 6 inches from the heat, turning and basting frequently. Test by pressing the meat with your finger. A slight springiness and resistance indicates medium-doneness in red meat. Brush again with the marinade and serve hot.

Yield: 4 servings

VARIATION
Boneless lamb from the shoulder may be used instead. Use 4- to 6-month-old lamb.

Pesto Frittata

A frittata is my free-form lazy way to cook on a Sunday morning, but it can also be schemed out on the drive home from work for an easy supper.

Consider these for fillings — new potatoes, red or green peppers, broccoli, green beans, carrots, cherry tomatoes, zucchini, Canadian bacon, mushrooms, shallots, chives, parsley, fresh herbs, and, of course, pesto.

Choose any 3 or 4 ingredients. Cut the vegetables to a uniform small size. Melt a little butter and oil in a sauté pan large enough for the frittata. Sauté the veggies briefly, stirring frequently. After a minute or two, add just a little water — a tablespoon or two. Partially cover the pan and steam over a low heat until the vegetables are tender crisp.

Thin about 2 tablespoons of pesto (Classic Basil, Mediterranean, Oregano, and Thyme pestos would all be good choices) with a little warm water or cream — a teaspoon or two — and dribble the pesto sauce over the vegetables in the pan.

Pour a few beaten eggs over the vegetables and scatter crumbled cheese and minced herbs or parsley over all. Cover the frittata and place in a 325°F. preheated oven for maybe 2 minutes or continue heating on the stove over low heat for about 2 minutes, just until set.

Serve hot in wedges, garnished with fresh herbs, parsley, or salsa.

Yield: 2 servings

Broccoli Fennel Souffle

2 cups sliced broccoli stems and
 florets
1 cup Fennel Pesto (page 16)
1/2 cup ricotta cheese
1/4 cup freshly grated Parmesan
 cheese
4 eggs, separated
Salt and freshly ground black
 pepper
1 tablespoon freshly grated
 Parmesan cheese

A gratin dish cooks a soufflé quickly and results in a browned crust and soft moist center.

Butter a 12-inch gratin dish or four 1-1/4 cup individual soufflés. Chill in the refrigerator.

Simmer the broccoli in boiling water to cover until just tender. Drain well. Set aside a few broccoli florets (about 1/2 cup).

Place the broccoli, pesto, ricotta, 1/4 cup Parmesan cheese, and egg yolks in a food processor or blender. Purée until combined. Taste and season generously. Add the reserved broccoli florets and process briefly, leaving some green pieces for texture.

Preheat the oven to 450°F.

In a separate bowl, whisk the egg whites just until they form soft peaks. Stir a third of the egg whites into the broccoli mixture;

then fold in the remainder, deflating the whites as little as possible.

Fill the gratin dish or small cups to the rim. Sprinkle with the remaining 1 tablespoon of Parmesan cheese. Place on a baking sheet. Bake the large soufflé approximately 15 to 18 minutes and the individual soufflés 10 to 12 minutes, until nicely browned and still moist in the center. Small soufflés can be unmolded, if desired, and served with a cheese sauce. Serve hot.

Yield: 4 servings

Eggplant Cannelloni

SAUCE

1/4 cup butter
1 tablespoon minced shallot
1/4 cup all-purpose unbleached
   flour
1-3/4 cups milk
1 teaspoon fresh marjoram or
   1/2 teaspoon dried
1/4 cup minced fresh parsley leaves
1/4 cup freshly grated Parmesan
   cheese
2 egg yolks
1-1/2 tablespoons Mediterranean
   Pesto (page 18)
Salt and freshly ground pepper

CANNELLONI

2 medium-size eggplants (about 3 to
   4 inches in diameter)
Approximately 1/4 cup olive oil
1/4 cup Classic Basil Pesto (page 7)
   or Winter Mediterranean Pesto
   (page 31)
1 large shallot, minced (1-1/2 to 2
   tablespoons)
2 cups whole milk ricotta cheese
   (1 pound)
1/2 cup chopped fresh parsley
   leaves
1/2 cup freshly grated Parmesan
   cheese
Salt and freshly ground pepper
6 ounces mozzarella cheese, thinly
   sliced
1 tablespoon fine bread crumbs
1 tablespoon freshly grated
   Parmesan cheese

To make the sauce, melt the butter in a sauté pan. Sauté the shallot until soft. Whisk in the flour. Then slowly whisk in the milk, stirring constantly. Add the marjoram, parsley, and grated Parmesan cheese. Cook over low heat.

In a small bowl, whisk the egg yolks, adding a tablespoon or two of the sauce. Combine with the sauce, but do not allow the sauce to come to a boil. Stir in the pesto and salt and pepper to taste. Remove from the heat.

To make the cannelloni, preheat the oven to 400°F.

Peel the eggplants and slice off the ends. Slice lengthwise into thin (about 3/8-inch) slices. Place close together on an oiled baking sheet. Brush the top side of each piece lightly with olive oil and bake for 10 minutes.

Reset the oven temperature to 350°F.

Heat the remaining oil in a sauté pan, and sauté the minced shallot for 2 minutes. Cool briefly and fold into the ricotta. Add the chopped parsley, 1/2 cup Parmesan cheese, salt, and pepper to taste.

With a spatula, spread some of the pesto on each eggplant slice. Cover with a slice of mozzarella on each. Place about 1 tablespoon of ricotta filling at the end of each eggplant slice and roll. Place seam side down in an oiled baking dish. Pour the sauce over the top. Sprinkle with bread crumbs and the remaining 1 tablespoon grated Parmesan cheese. Bake covered for 25 minutes. Uncover and bake until lightly browned, about 10 minutes. Serve hot or warm.

Yield: 4 to 6 servings

Pesto Pizza

DOUGH

1 envelope dry baker's yeast
1/2 teaspoon sugar
3/4 cup warm water
2 tablespoons olive oil
2 cups unbleached all-purpose flour
1/2 teaspoon salt

TOPPING

3/4 cup any basil pesto (pages 7 to 14) or Mediterranean Pesto (page 18) or Oregano Thyme Pesto (page 28)
2 cups grated whole milk mozzarella cheese
About 3 tablespoons freshly grated Parmesan cheese
4 sun-dried tomatoes in oil (page 126), drained and cut into julienne slivers (optional)
Cornmeal or a little flour for pizza paddle

Baking pizzas in the oven on unglazed floor tiles (4 tiles will cost about $4) or a pizza stone (which costs about $27) simulates a brick oven, producing a nice brown crust. This thin crisp pizza is easily made and makes a fine appetizer or entrée.

In a small bowl combine the yeast, sugar, warm water, and olive oil. Stir to mix.

Combine the flour and salt in a food processor. Process a few seconds to blend. With the motor running, slowly add the yeast mixture through the feed tube and continue to process until a smooth, elastic dough ball is formed. If the dough is too sticky, add a tablespoon or 2 of flour; if too dry, add water by the tablespoon. A soft, moist dough will produce a good pizza crust.

If mixing the dough by hand, combine the flour and salt in a medium-size bowl. Add the yeast mixture and stir with a wooden spoon until the dough can be gathered into a ball. Turn onto a floured board and knead until the dough is smooth and elastic, about 10 minutes.

Wrap the dough in lightly oiled plastic wrap and set aside. The dough may be made ahead and refrigerated up to 1 day.

Place the unglazed tiles or a pizza stone (you could also use a cast-iron frying pan set upside down) on the lowest shelf of the oven. Center a lining of heavy foil on the floor of the oven to catch any cornmeal or flour spills. Preheat the oven to 500°F. for 10 minutes. Dust a wooden pizza paddle (or baking sheet without sides) lightly with cornmeal or flour to slide the pizza into the oven and to remove it from the oven when done.

Divide the dough into 4 equal portions. Flatten a dough ball and roll on a lightly floured board to about 1/8 or 1/4 inch thick and about 10 inches in diameter. Transfer the pizza to the paddle or baking sheet. Spread 2 to 3 tablespoons of pesto to within 3/4 or 1 inch of the edge of the dough. Sprinkle the pesto with about 1/2 cup grated mozzarella cheese and 2 teaspoons or more of grated Parmesan cheese. If using sun-dried tomatoes, scatter the slivers over the top. Shake the paddle to be sure the dough slides freely. Slide the pizza onto the preheated tiles or stone with a quick wrist motion. Bake for 7 to 9 minutes until the bottom crust is crisp and brown. The crust will soften a bit as it cools. Remove from the oven with the pizza paddle. Repeat with the remaining dough and filling. Serve immediately.

Yield: four 10-inch pizzas

Calzone with Herbed Vegetables

DOUGH

2 tablespoons dry yeast
1 teaspoon sugar
1-1/3 cups warm water (105-115°)
4 cups unbleached all-purpose flour
2 tablespoons olive oil
1 teaspoon salt

FILLING

1-1/2 cups grated sharp cheddar
   cheese (6 ounces)
1-1/2 cups grated (cold) mozzarella
   cheese (6 ounces)
3 tablespoons unbleached all--
   purpose flour
2 tablespoons olive oil
1 medium-size onion, roughly
   chopped
2 small summer squash, roughly
   chopped (about 2 cups)

1 large stalk of broccoli, roughly
   chopped (about 2 cups)
1 small red pepper, sliced
2 tablespoons unbleached all--
   purpose flour
1/4 cup (or more to taste) Basil and
   Oregano Pesto (page 9),
   Oregano Thyme Pesto (page 28),
   Oregano Pesto (page 19), Thyme
   Pesto (page 27), or Winter
   Mediterranean Pesto (page 31)
2 tablespoons freshly grated
   Parmesan cheese
Salt and pepper
1 egg
2 tablespoons milk
Vegetable oil
2 tablespoons cornmeal

Calzones are good versatile pizza fare. The combination of herb pestos with vegetables and cheeses is a natural.

To make the dough, dissolve the yeast and sugar in the warm water. Let sit for about 5 minutes or until bubbly.

Add the flour, olive oil, and salt. Run the processor to knead for 2 minutes, or mix in a bowl and knead by hand for about 10 minutes.

Place the dough in an oiled bowl. Turn to coat with the oil. Cover and let rise in a warm place until double, about 1 hour.

While the dough rises, make the filling. Toss the grated cheeses with the 3 tablespoons flour. Set aside.

Heat the olive oil in a sauté pan. Sauté the chopped onion for 2 to 3 minutes, just until it begins to soften. Remove from the heat. Combine with the remaining vegetables and flour. Add the pesto and Parmesan cheese. Combine with the grated cheeses and season to taste with salt and pepper. Add more pesto to taste.

Preheat the oven to 450°F. Beat together the egg and milk to make an egg wash.

Punch down the dough. Divide the dough into 8 balls. Roll out each into a circle about 1/4 inch thick. Place about 1/2 cup filling on half the dough, leaving a 1/2 inch border. Moisten the edge of the dough with water. Fold half the dough over the filling so that the edges meet, pinching as you go to form a fluted edge and seal the filling within. Brush the top lightly with the egg wash. Cut 2 small slashes for steam vents on top. Use all the dough and filling in this fashion.

Oil a ceramic cooking stone or pizza pan (preferably a black one) and sprinkle with cornmeal. Place the calzones on the prepared pan. Place the pan near the bottom of the oven. Bake for 20 to 25 minutes until very brown and crisp. Serve hot.

Yield: 8 calzones

5.
More Sauces

Pesto Hollandaise

3 egg yolks
1-1/2 tablespoons fresh lemon juice
1/8 teaspoon salt
1/4 cup melted butter
1/4 cup Classic Basil Pesto (page 7)

This is a lovely sauce for poached fish and broccoli. Try it with asparagus in Eggs Benedict.

Combine the egg yolks, lemon juice, and salt in a blender. Blend for 5 seconds. Heat the butter to boiling in a small saucepan. Add the pesto to the butter and heat until sizzling hot, stirring constantly. Do not brown. Remove from the heat. With the blender running, slowly add the hot butter pesto mixture to the egg yolks. Taste and adjust for seasoning. Serve immediately. The green color will diminish if the sauce is held.

Yield: About 3/4 cup

Crème Fraîche

1 cup heavy cream
1 teaspoon buttermilk

Crème fraîche is a versatile thickening agent to have on hand. It is delicious with fresh berries or fruit. Crème fraîche is also known as French dairy cream.

Combine the cream and buttermilk in a covered glass jar. Let stand at room temperature until thickened, about 24 hours, then refrigerate. It will keep for a week or two and continue to thicken. If you wish, add more cream to continue the culture.

Yield: 1 cup

Appendices

Sun-dried Italian Plum Tomatoes

5 pounds ripe Italian plum
   tomatoes
Salt
Olive oil to fill jars (about 1-1/4
   cups)
Herbs (5 or 6 fresh basil leaves, or
   2 or 3 fresh 2-inch sprigs of
   oregano and 2 or 3 fresh 2-inch
   sprigs of thyme, or 8 peppercorns
   and 6 fresh 2-inch sprigs of
   thyme)

Once you have tasted your first sun-dried Italian plum tomatoes in a dish, you will probably want to add them to your flavoring repertoire. In fact, they are a necessary ingredient for making Red Basil Pesto (page 8).

During the drying process, the natural sweetness and flavor of the ripe tomatoes are intensified. Then the tomatoes are packed with herbs and olive oil. The result is wonderful flavor, and just 2 tablespoons of the chopped tomatoes can transform an ordinary dish into something quite special. The oil in which the tomatoes are packed is also very flavorful and can be used in vegetable sautés.

Although specialty food stores and mail order food companies now sell these tomatoes, the price is quite dear. A 10-1/2 ounce jar, which contains about 7 ounces of tomatoes, will cost over $10.

If you grow your own tomatoes, you will find it is well worth the effort to make your own sun-dried Italian plum tomatoes. And, by making your own, you can vary the flavors, using basil, oregano, thyme — or whatever herb combinations strike your fancy.

Despite the name, the flavor of these tomatoes is just fine if you dry the tomatoes in a food dryer or oven. If you live in a dry, sunny climate, you can dry the tomatoes in the sun, as you dry other fruits. Then proceed with the recipe given below. This recipe makes 3 half-pint jars.

Select perfect ripe Italian plum tomatoes or another small fleshy tomato variety. Slice each tomato almost in half vertically and open like a book. Remove the stem end with a small V cut and cut off any blemishes. You may dry the tomatoes in this form, or you can remove the pulp and seeds to reduce the drying time.

To dry in a food dryer, place the open tomatoes skin side down on drying racks. Salt them lightly; this helps to draw out the moisture. Space the drying racks in the food dryer about 2-1/2 inches apart. Set on high heat and dry for 10 to 16 hours, until the tomato halves are leathery but not dry or hard. Small tomatoes will dry quicker than large ones. Check the dryer at intervals and remove the tomatoes individually as they reach the leathery stage.

To dry in the oven, preheat the oven to 200°F. Place the tomatoes on racks on baking sheets (probably 2 large cookie sheets will be needed). Salt the tomatoes lightly. Bake for about 6 to 7 hours. Switch the baking sheets from top to bottom after a few hours, and remove the smaller tomatoes as they dry.

Cool slightly. Fold the tomato halves

closed. Pack very tightly in half-pint jars, inserting the sprigs of fresh herbs between the tomatoes. I find it easiest to pack the tomatoes upright and to make 2 layers of tomatoes with herbs in each layer. Add olive oil to completely cover the tomatoes. Poke a knife in around the edges to let any air bubbles escape. Seal the jars tightly.

Store at room temperature for 6 weeks to allow the flavors to develop.

A Culinary Tour of Herbs

There's no question that Americans are discovering new ways to prepare foods with herbs. Thai food, Mexican, Indian, Vietnamese, Szechwan are some of the cuisines enthusiastically embraced by imaginative cooks. In response, stores are stocking lemon grass, cilantro, various hot peppers and spices, fresh ginger, shitake and wild mushrooms, and many fresh herbs. Fresh basil, tarragon, thyme, dill and rosemary can be shipped anywhere, at a price, year-round, even here in northern Vermont.

Despite the new availability of fresh herbs from stores, fresh herbs from your own garden still provide the greatest reward. The space requirement for an herb garden is small, and the cost is minimal in terms of both time and budget. Herb plants are worked easily into a pleasing landscape scheme, and neglected corners can be transformed into permanent perennial herb beds with very little effort. Creeping thyme, with its beautiful blossoms, or opal basil with parsley plants, make a delightful garden border. Many herbs grow in almost a wild state and will cover large areas and hillsides. Marjoram, the mints, creeping thymes, oregano, sage, and tansy are a few of the perennials that spread and require almost no care, returning year after year. Here is a tour of the primary pesto herbs that are easy to grow and harvest.

Basil

All along the Mediterranean sea, the sunny hillsides are covered with a small-leafed basil, and people gather the herb at will. Pots of bush basil plants decorate the balconies and open windows, acting as a fly deterrent for unscreened windows, as well as serving culinary needs.

Basil is one of the earliest known herbs.

Herbalists report about 150 species. The seeds probably were carried from India or Thailand west to Babylon with the early traders. There are many ancient folk tales associated with this king of herbs, with scorpions, love potents, and madness frequenting the superstitions. According to legend, only the king with a golden sword may make the first cutting.

In mild climates, a basil plant is a semiwoody perennial shrub. But botanists generally classify sweet basil as an annual, and new plants are germinated from seed. (See Appendix III for sources of mail order seeds.) The seeds germinate quickly in 2 or 3 days under warm conditions (70 to 75°F.). Basil can be propagated from the stem cuttings of firm wood, but it is hardly worth the effort. Basil is so easily grown from seed, it can be planted in thick patches or rows as you would plant any other green. It makes an excellent succession crop for early spinach.

Of all the culinary varieties of interest to the basil lover, **sweet basil** *(Ocimum basilicum)* is the most commonly known. It is a fast-growing annual, easily grown from seed sown in the late spring, after all danger of frost has passed. Regular cuttings are usually made throughout the growing season by cutting the stems back to the second set of leaves as soon as the flower buds begin to form, and continuing the cuttings at 2 or 3 week intervals. Some gardeners sow continuous plantings of basil and harvest the entire plant to obtain young sweet leaves. For the best flavor, the basil should not be allowed to flower.

Lettuce leaf basil produces the most abundant harvest. The leaves are 3 to 4 inches long and almost as wide. The leaf surfaces are puckered and wavy, and the large leaf is somewhat convex. It makes a fine pesto, and the large leaf can be used as a wrapper for finger foods.

Piccolo verde fino basil is reputed to be the true authentic pesto basil. The glossy green narrow leaves are about 2 inches long on a tall (2-1/2 foot), strong growing plant. Piccolo's flavor is sweet with a complex, light aroma.

Dark opal basil is a beautiful ornamental and culinary herb. Plant it with parsley plants along a garden border. This purple basil makes a delicious red pesto (see page 8). Use it to make herb vinegar, add it to salads, and use it as a colorful garnish.

French fine leaf basil is a favorite with French cooks. It is a freely branching tender perennial, characterized by many tiny green leaves, and well suited to pot culture. The plant can live for years if it is pruned and repotted regularly. The sweet minty flavor makes a good pesto, but the task of picking the many small leaves may deter the pesto maker.

The small **bush basil** from the Mediterranean is a compact miniature plant, also well suited for pot culture. The leaves are sweet and a little clove-like in flavor. Since the leaves are small, it takes a number of plants to produce enough for pesto.

Holy basil is very pungent and rather spicy in aroma. Varieties are common in India and Thailand, and strains of the plant go back to biblical times. It makes an unusual and interesting pesto.

Lemon basil was introduced to this country from Thailand by the Department of Agriculture in 1940. This lemon-scented basil has been in cultivation since the 16th century in England. The leaves are a light green and lack the glossy surface of the sweet basil leaves. I prefer it as a cutting herb for cooking, the citrusy basil flavor is quite nice in pestos.

Basil stems and flower stalks have almost as much flavor as the leaves. After removing the leaves, add the stems and flower stalks to stews and soups, and throw them on the grill for a wonderful premeating aroma. The flowers are sweet and make a terrific basil-flower vinegar.

Cilantro

Cilantro, or coriander *(Coriandrum sativum),* also known as Chinese parsley, is a tall (2-foot) annual with lower leaves that resemble flat-leafed Italian parsley and feathery upper foliage that resembles anise. The plant has pretty white blooms and aromatic brown seeds with an outer shell. The smoky-flavored green leaves are used frequently in warm climate cuisines on several continents. Cilantro is an herb of choice in California and the Southwest. Successive plantings are recommended for steady foliage.

Fennel

An annual that is grown for its bulbous base and anise celery flavor is **Florence fennel.** The feathery upper leaves can be added to salads, or chopped and frozen in ice cubes for later use. Lay fresh fennel branches on the grill when broiling fish.

Garlic Chives

A handsome plant worth growing in the herb garden for its bloom as well as flavor is **garlic chives** *(Allium tuberosum).* This perennial is slow-growing, with long chive leaves that are flat, instead of hollow. The tall large flower heads have many white star-shaped small flowers that bloom from August through September in the North.

Mint

All the mints are hardy perennials and rampant growers. They need to be contained within the garden. Propagation is usually by runners or cuttings. **Peppermint** *(Mentha peperita)* has dark green leaves with purple tones. The stems are usually purple, and the plant has a pervasive minty aroma that makes an excellent pesto. **Spearmint** *(Mentha spicata)* has narrow pointed bright green veined leaves and often grows to 3 feet in height. Spearmint is an old-fashioned favorite, used for mint sauces, iced tea, and juleps. **English mint,** *(Mentha cordifolia),* with small crinkly leaves, may be harder to locate. It has an excellent flavor and is well worth looking for.

Oregano

Another herb with variations in taste and pungency is oregano. The low-growing **Greek oregano** or the taller **Italian oregano** are the most flavorful varieties for culinary purposes. **Wild Marjoram,** frequently sold as oregano, has very little flavor for cooking, although the small pink flowers are delightful in a dried bouquet.

Rosemary

There are many varieties of rosemary, from tall woody shrubs and bonzai-like plants to creeping ground covers. A tender perennial, rosemary may grow to be a 4-foot or 5-foot-tall bush in temperate climates. Where winter temperatures drop below 10°F., the herb can be grown as a pot plant for summers outside and winters indoors. Rosemary can be propagated from cuttings and by layering. Seed germination and plant growth are slow. *Rosemarinus officinalis* is a tall upright plant with dark green needles and strong growth. Two favorite varieties are the tall **Miss Jessup rosemary** with golden green needles and **trailing rosemary** *(R. officinalis prostrata)* with prostrate trailing recurving branches that grow in interesting shapes.

Sage

Sage *(Salvia officinalis)* is a hardy perennial, often growing to 2½ feet in height. The **garden sage** variety with grey-green leaves is most often used for culinary purposes. It is easy to grow from seed and usually grows as wide as it is tall. The golden, purple, and tricolor forms also may be used for cooking, but they are not as hardy as the green garden sage. Sage continues to grow well with frequent clippings. The leaves make an attractive garnish.

Tarragon

Tarragon presents a problem for the herbalist. For culinary purposes, it is crucial to get divisions of **French tarragon** *(Artemisia dranunculus)* with its tangy anise-flavored overtones. The plant is propagated by divisions of the root of second-year plants, or from cuttings taken in mid-summer. The cuttings take about 2 months to root and must be carried through the winter for spring planting. **Russian tarragon** grown from seed has very little flavor. The demand for French tarragon, recently, far exceeds the supply of plants.

Thyme

Of the thymes, the most noteworthy for culinary purposes are the upright forms of common thyme *(Thymus vulgaris).* **French thyme** with narrow pointed grayish green leaves and small lavender flowers is the most frequently used, since it germinates easily from seed. The broader-leafed **English thyme,** or **winter thyme,** has dark green leaves and a similar flavor, with small pink or lavender flowers. It is difficult to germinate from seed. Division of the established plants in early spring or propagation by cuttings are the recommended methods for starting new plants.

Lemon thyme *(Thymus citriodorus),* with glossy rounded leaves on a compact bush, has a lemon scent and taste. Propagate this hardy perennial by cuttings or division of the whole plant.

Orange balsam thyme has a distinct citrus pine scent and taste, with narrow sparse leaves on a small upright plant. This thyme is also propagated by cuttings or division of the whole plant.

The creeping thymes, small ground cover plants, are usually grown as ornamentals in banks and rock gardens or between flagstones. Their many colored masses of flowers range from purple through red, lavender, pink, and white. Of culinary interest for their unique flavors are **caraway thyme** and **oregano thyme.** The small, tight, ground-hugging caraway thyme forms a mat about 6 inches wide, with very small, shiny, narrow-pointed leaves. With its pink flowers and caraway flavor, it is a delightful little plant. Oregano thyme forms an 8-inch-wide mat, with rounded green leaves shaded with mahogany. The flavor is an aromatic cross between oregano and thyme.

Harvesting Herbs

The time to harvest herbs is when the volatile oils, from which the aroma comes, are at their peak. This is when the flower buds first appear, but are not yet open.

Harvesting should be done with a sharp knife or with pruning shears. If the herb you are harvesting is an annual, cut off the top half of the stem. Basil should be cut back to the second set of leaves. You will probably want to harvest fast-growing annuals, such as basil, at 2-week or 3-week intervals during the prime growing season. Plan to make pesto while your herbs are at their peak. Here in the North, as Labor Day approaches with cooler night temperatures and less intense sunlight, the basil leaves lose flavor. Sweet basil loves plenty of heat and light.

Perennial leafy herbs should not be cut as severely as annuals. Usually cutting a third of a perennial's growth will not injure a well-established plant. Harvest only small amounts from young plants. As you harvest from a perennial, consider the shape of the plant; you are actually pruning as well as harvesting.

Harvest early in the day, after the dew has dried, but before the hot noon sun has a chance to wilt the leaves. Handle the leaves carefully to keep the oil glands on the surface of the leaves intact. This is especially important with basil. Place the freshly cut leaves in shallow baskets as you pick; don't pack them tightly. Pick healthy foliage and discard the damaged leaves.

Sometimes the herbs will require washing before they can be dried. You can avoid this by gently spraying the leafy herbs with water the day before you plan to harvest. The leaves will be washed free of any soil that has splashed up on their surface and will have time to dry. If necessary, wash harvested herbs by immersing the whole stems in water and swishing gently. Then dry on towels.

If you plan to use your harvested herbs fresh, place the stems in 2 or 3 inches of water in a tall container. Loosely cover the leaves with a large plastic bag or plastic wrap and store in a cool place or refrigerate. The herbs will stay fresh for about a week.

To dry herbs, tie them together in small bundles and hang them upside down to dry in a dark, airy room. They will be dry in 10 to 14 days in the summer. Strip the leaves from the stems and store them in tightly capped containers away from the heat of the stove.

INDEX

To receive a current catalog from
The Crossing Press,
please call toll-free,
800-777-1048.
Visit our Website on the Internet at:
www.crossingpress.com